Hans Bethe, Prophet of Energy

HANS BETHE, PROPHET OF ENERGY

Jeremy Bernstein

BASIC BOOKS, INC., PUBLISHERS

NEW YORK

The text originally appeared in *The New Yorker*.

The drawing on page iii is by Silverman
© 1979, The New Yorker Magazine, Inc.

Library of Congress Cataloging in Publication Data

Bernstein, Jeremy, 1929–
  Hans Bethe, prophet of energy.

  Based on articles written for the New Yorker.
  Bibliography: p. 203
  Includes index.
  1. Bethe, Hans Albrecht, 1906–
2. Physicists—Biography. 3. Atomic energy—
History. I. Title.
QC16.B46B47   539'.092'4 [B]   80–50555
ISBN: 0–465–02903–5

Copyright © 1980 by Jeremy Bernstein
Printed in the United States of America
DESIGNED BY VINCENT TORRE
10 9 8 7 6 5 4 3 2 1

Contents

Preface

In the fall of 1977 I decided to attempt a profile of Hans
Bethe. At the time I was not well acquainted with Bethe,
though I *did* know something about his work. During the
entire period when I was learning about the theory of elementary particles and nuclear physics I had Bethe's books
and review articles before me, some of which I all but knew
by heart. So, I believe, did most of the theoretical physicists
of my generation. I also knew something of Bethe's character and intellectual integrity. He seemed to me to be an
outstanding example of how a scientist can and should react
when confronted with extremely difficult questions of public policy. I hope that the reader of this book will come to
understand what this means. In any event, I wrote to him
to ask if he would have the time to work with me on a
profile for *The New Yorker*. He accepted but added a

caveat, "I should like to warn you that my personal life is not terribly interesting. . . . Possibly after the first interview you will come to the conclusion that I am really not very interesting, and in that case please feel free to stop right there." This book is a result of a series of interviews that began in November of 1977 and continued, sometimes by visits, sometimes over the telephone, often by letters, for two years. Indeed, in the technical aspects of this profile, the work became more like a scientific collaboration than a series of interviews.

To understand why one would devote this much time to a profile I should explain what I have always believed a biographical study of a scientist should be. The center of gravity of a working scientist is his work. Anyone who has engaged in scientific research, however modest, knows that while it is going on, everything else ebbs and flows in terms of how the work is progressing. There is an anecdote about the great Austrian theoretical physicist Wolfgang Pauli that nicely illustrates the point. Before the advent of the discovery of "spin," in the middle nineteen-twenties, Pauli was attempting to explain a subtle effect in atomic spectra which could not, as it turned out, be explained without the notion of spin. Imagine, then, Pauli's frustration in trying to describe something in a language that, as yet, did not contain the word or the sequences of words needed to describe it. At the time, Pauli was visiting Niels Bohr's institute in Copenhagen and, in his frustration, would take long evening walks near the waterfront. One evening, as he was trudging along despondently near the water, he was surprised to hear an elderly lady say to him, "Don't jump in, young man . . . no woman is worth committing suicide over." The work of a scientist is both his elixir and millstone. Hence, any biography of a scientist which does not focus on his ideas is, in my view, a misspent opportunity.

Preface

Bethe's work has ranged over so many fields of modern physics and astrophysics that it would take a textbook, not a profile, to do justice to it, although I hope that by the end of the book the reader will get some sense of the enterprise. (In the bibliography I give a few references that allow the interested reader to dig deeper.) But the real point of this book, and of *The New Yorker* articles in which it originated, is the examination of what may well be the most significant question today concerning both science and public policy; namely that of energy. What one learns as one begins to examine this problem is that everything is connected to everything. Technology is only one aspect of the energy problem and it cannot be separated from politics or economics, or from the most fundamental questions of existence that now confront the present and future generations.

In a matter this complex it seems to me that the first order of business is to try to establish the facts. How much? How many? Where? How does it work? Can it be built? While the reader may not agree with the final conclusions of how to deal with the energy dilemma, he or she, I believe, can have confidence that the facts presented are objective and the best that could be obtained—irrespective of whether they support any particular point of view. But these facts were not easy to come by. This has to do, in part, with the difficulty of making estimates of natural resources and the like, and with the fact that the data have enormous economic implications for both governments and industries. Consequently, one must attempt to sift through the available information to arrive at something like an objective statement. One is on firmer ground traversing the realm of science—trying, for example, to describe how a nuclear reactor works. But we are on less firm ground when

Preface

we attempt to describe how one of these technological constructions can fail to work. So many types of failure are imaginable and their consequences so different that again one is forced to fall back on statistical estimates and educated conjecture. Someone who insists on a no-risk, absolute certainty in these matters, is, in my view, simply refusing to live in the real world. I put in the same category critics of a particular technology—say, of nuclear power—who, while bemoaning the expense or the dangers, do not provide a program of detailed alternate solutions. It is not enough to say "go solar," use "windmills," or "find geothermal sources" unless the proposer will tell us where, how much, and what it will cost. Once the discussion becomes quantitative one can, at least, begin to examine the assumptions, and to see if there is a consensus.

In preparing the book I have been aided by many people who wrote to me with specific suggestions and criticisms after my articles appeared. Scientists are used to this kind of give and take and, indeed, welcome it. And I have made every effort to be responsive to these critics. While a long list of acknowledgments is often as tedious to read as the want ad pages of a newspaper I could not, as a matter of conscience, allow these helpful and generous people to go unacknowledged.

First of all, I am indebted to both Hans and Rose Bethe. The Bethes are two of the busiest people on earth. But despite this, they responded to an all but infinite number of questions for two years. Without their help there could not have been a book. I also received generous help from many of my colleagues. I would like to mention some of them. Both Gerald Feinberg and Freeman Dyson made numerous critical suggestions and some of the numbers in the book were worked out with Feinberg. Sir Rudolf and

Preface

Genia Peierls aided and entertained me by reminiscing about the early days. A. David Rossin and Lester Berkowitz, both nuclear engineers, attempted to educate me about reactors. A number of my colleagues at the Aspen Center for Physics read the articles in various drafts, and H. H. Barschall, S. Chandrasekhar, and W. Frank made some very important suggestions for the book. In addition I owe an enormous debt to members of the staff of *The New Yorker*. Pat Crow, my editor, put up with revisions that would have driven anyone else to despair. Richard Sacks and Sara Spencer made a heroic effort to check all of the facts. Finally, there is, of course, William Shawn. It was Mr. Shawn's conviction that all sides of the energy question should have a hearing in *The New Yorker*. My writing about science for the general public is a reflection of his conviction that it should be done, and the articles and this book are a testimonial to his concern.

Jeremy Bernstein, July 1980

PART I

The Early Years

Chapter 1

German Beginnings

UNTIL the advent of nuclear fission a few decades ago, all the energy sources that the human race made use of could ultimately be traced back to the sun. Coal, oil, gas, wood—the things we burn—are things that once grew or still grow, and the fuel of growth is sunlight. Today, we make a small amount of our electricity by directly converting the radiant energy of the sun, and in the next century a sizable fraction of it may be made that way. Most of the rest of our electricity production can be traced back indirectly to the effects of solar energy. In view of this fact, it is remarkable that few of us know what solar energy is and how it is produced. The lack of specific knowledge about this and all sorts of other matters is part—and a very important part—of what vexes our present collective thinking about energy. What makes the sun shine?

3

I / The Early Years

What is a nuclear reactor, and how does it generate power? What is nuclear fusion, and how could *it* be used to generate power? How much coal do we use each year, and what would be the consequences for the earth and for man if we needed to use four times as much? Where is that coal to be found, and where would it have to be shipped? What is nuclear waste, and how much does a power reactor produce each year? What are the costs of energy? What are the numbers? How much? How many? How big? Where?

Because most people lack such information and understanding, the discussion of the energy question has become a "debate," and as the energy crisis deepens, this debate becomes more rancorous and less informed. What is needed is not rhetoric but information and understanding. To compound the confusion, not even the experts always agree. Some of the problems involved with energy *are* open to disagreement; knowledgeable people can arrive at different conclusions. But this does not mean that no generally accepted scientific information exists; indeed, many scientists are now spending much of their time and effort trying to share such information with the public. In this enterprise, no individual has been more active than the seventy-four-year-old Nobel laureate Hans Albrecht Bethe. Bethe writes and lectures tirelessly about energy. His office, at Cornell University, where he is professor emeritus, is, he says, "a filing cabinet" for documents on energy, which he reads, criticizes, and evaluates for scientists all over the world. Bethe's interest in energy goes back a long way. In 1938, he discovered the specific mechanisms that generate stellar energy, and it was for this work that he was awarded the Nobel Prize in Physics in 1967. Bethe, who was thirty-one when he began working on the problem of solar energy, came to the United States in 1935 to teach at Cornell. By that time, he had already done basic work in several areas of theoretical physics, and today the list of his accomplishments is all but incredible. A few months after his sixtieth birthday, Bethe was presented with a book entitled "Perspectives in Modern Physics," which was written in his honor; it contains forty-one essays by various scientists, on subjects ranging from earthquakes to every conceivable branch of pure physics. Bethe has made fundamental original contributions to each of the disciplines that make up the subject matter of these essays. In addition, he has written, with collaborators, several books and three monumental review articles—one on atomic physics, one on solid-state physics, and one on nuclear physics. The article on nuclear physics, which appeared in three installments in *Reviews of Modern Physics* in 1936 and 1937 and became known informally as Bethe's Bible, was the first comprehensive treatment of the subject ever to appear in print. A routine review article is just that—a review, or summary, of published work. But Bethe's review articles went well beyond that. Wherever he found gaps in the literature, he filled them in. When he felt that the work of other physicists was incomplete or unclear, he redid it. He simply recreated the subject.

In commenting on these reviews and on Bethe's work in general, his colleagues R. F. Bacher, who is professor emeritus at the California Institute of Technology, and V. F. Weisskopf, who is professor emeritus at the Massachusetts Institute of Technology and was formerly the director-general of the international nuclear laboratory Conseil Européen pour la Recherche Nucléaire (CERN), in Geneva, wrote, in a joint introduction to Bethe's birthday book:

The three great reviews are characteristic of Bethe's broad and encyclopedic knowledge but they by no means give a complete picture of it. His interests cover a much broader horizon. Bethe steps in productively whenever a new physical phenomenon is discovered. He is among the first with an exhaustive explanation on the basis of the latest theoretical ideas; or whenever a new theoretical method is conceived, he is among the first with an exhaustive application to some yet unexplained observations. He has his own personal way of simple and direct approach to theory and experiment and his typical trademark of thoroughness. It is all "handmade." He does not take the experimental results for granted. He analyzes them himself, often making corrections for effects that had been overlooked, and taking great pains in numerical work, in fitting curves, and in estimating errors.

They commented:

We live in an industrial age today wherein craftsmanship is becoming a lost art. Specialization is the order of the day. Where is the man who can work with his own hands on any kind of material and create a finished product which reflects his insight and knowledge and bears his personal mark? The great craftsman of our profession, the master of the trade, is Hans Bethe.

In view of Bethe's reputation, it was hardly surprising that in 1943, when J. Robert Oppenheimer, the director of the Los Alamos atomic-bomb project, became convinced that the complexity of the work would require the creation of specialized divisions at the laboratory, he appointed Bethe to head the Theoretical Division. In 1946, Bethe was awarded the President's Medal of Merit for his work at Los Alamos. In 1955, he received the Max Planck Medal, given by the German Physical Society, for outstanding research in modern theoretical physics. In 1961, he received the Enrico Fermi Award, given by the United States Atomic Energy Commission, for his work at Los Alamos and also for his general work on nuclear theory. And six years later came the Nobel Prize in Physics.

Bethe (the name is pronounced like the Greek "beta") was born in Strasbourg, in Alsace-Lorraine, on July 2, 1906. "My father was a physiologist," Bethe told me. "At the time of my birth, he was a *Privatdozent* at the University of Strasbourg"—a postdoctoral instructor whose only remuneration was the fees he could collect directly by lecturing to students. "He had come from Stettin, an old city on the Oder River, in what was then the northern Prussian province of Pomerania and is now part of Poland," Bethe went on. "His family had been in that area for many centuries; the family records can be traced back to the Thirty Years' War—1640 or thereabouts. The previous records are lost, like most records in areas fought over in that war. My father's family was Protestant, and through history some members were Protestant ministers, and some were schoolteachers. My grandfather was a medical doctor —the closest anyone in that family had come to being a scientist. My oldest uncle, whom we called the Greek Uncle, was a professor of Greek at the University of Leipzig. The second son became a doctor, like his father; the third son went into business—unfortunately, not successfully. My father was the youngest child; my aunt, Tante Lisbeth, the oldest."

Bethe said, "My father was quite a rebellious boy. He ran away from home—I think at the age of fifteen—to join a circus. He wanted to become a juggler, but after two or three weeks he found out that it was really hard to become a juggler, so he came home. It took my grandfather a long time to forgive him. He punished the runaway by not speaking to him for several weeks. My father was interested in the natural sciences from a very early age. He was not

7

I / The Early Years

at all interested in schoolwork; four times during his school years, he failed to be promoted. Later on, he always used to mention this to comfort the parents of similar children. Anyway, he made up for it. After he finally graduated from a *Gymnasium*, at the age of twenty, he studied intensively, and three years later he had his Ph.D. in zoology from the University of Munich. Then he went to Strasbourg to do physiology. He was told that he ought to take a medical degree in addition, and did so, but I don't believe he really studied hard for it. I think he got the degree on the basis of his published papers, and not because of the clinical work he did."

Bethe continued, "My mother's family was Jewish. Her father was a professor at the University of Strasbourg; his specialty was ear, nose, and throat diseases. For a Jew to get such a professorship was at that time—around 1880— quite exceptional. His family had been grape growers and wine merchants in the Palatinate. My grandmother came from a family of cloth merchants."

Because theoretical physicists and mathematicians are famous for their mathematical precocity, I asked Bethe if he had any early mathematical memories.

"Oh, yes—many," he replied. "I was interested in numbers from a very early age. When I was five, I said to my mother on a walk one day, 'Isn't it strange that if a zero comes at the end of a number it means a lot but if it is at the beginning of a number it doesn't mean anything?' And one day when I was about four, Richard Ewald, a professor of physiology, who was my father's boss, asked me on the street, 'What is point five divided by two?' I answered, 'Dear Uncle Ewald, that I don't know,' but the next time I saw him I ran to him and said, 'Uncle Ewald, it's point two-five.' I knew about decimals then. When I was seven,

I learned about powers, and filled a whole book with the powers of two and three."

In 1912, the Bethes moved from Strasbourg to Kiel, where Bethe's father became chairman of the Physiology Department at the University of Kiel, and then, in 1915, they moved on to Frankfurt, for Bethe's father had been invited to start a Department of Physiology at the University of Frankfurt, which had been founded only the year before. Bethe, who was a rather frail child, was kept out of a regular school until the family moved to Frankfurt. In Kiel, he had been one of a small group of children studying under a private tutor. "Before starting with the tutor, I knew how to read and write," Bethe recalled. "But I wrote in a very funny way—only in capital letters and from left to right for the first line and then from right to left for the next line, and so on. Years later, I discovered, on the island of Crete, that there are many Greek inscriptions written the same way. At Teacher Lass's—the tutor's—I learned proper writing. I think I went to his house for two hours three days a week, so it was not very time-consuming. My life in Kiel was free and easy, but I had almost no friends. I saw the other children at Teacher Lass's, and I quite liked them, but I had no real friendships with them. My life was spent almost entirely with grown-ups—with my parents and close relatives. There was a lot of solitary contemplation. My father did talk to me about scientific things. He knew a bit of mathematics—mainly algebra—and in his work he used a slide rule. He had learned calculus, but could not apply it; at least, though, he understood what it was about. On the whole, my father was concerned that I should not work too far ahead of the school curriculum for my age, so when I wanted to read his book on trigonometry and calculus I had to borrow it secretly. But by then I was fourteen, and nowadays many mathematically bright youngsters learn calculus at that age."

In Frankfurt, Bethe began to attend a regular school—a *Gymnasium*. "They gave me an entrance examination that was very easy," he recalled. "The *Gymnasium* was for me, in the beginning, a strange new environment. All those boys—I think there were about forty in the class, some of them quite rough. I was new to Frankfurt and to the school—to *any* school. I was lucky in the end, because about three of the boys liked me and became my friends. It could have been very different. I did not suffer any beatings, or anything—I just felt myself a stranger in this group. I was perhaps a quarter of a year younger than the normal age for my class, but we were all about nine years old. Many of the boys were very good in gym, which I was not. I had never done any physical exercise to speak of, so I was very, very bad in gym. I always got a D in gym, and I've stayed that way, except that I have learned to ski and to climb mountains, both of which give me great pleasure."

I asked Bethe if his mathematical ability had been recognized in the *Gymnasium*.

"Not right away," he replied. "In fact, I think the recognition didn't come until I was in about my sixth year of the *Gymnasium*, which had nine years altogether. Then the math teacher noticed that maybe I was a little out of the ordinary. But he completely failed to understand what I was good at. When he wanted to give me some more advanced work, he asked me to prove a rather difficult theorem in plane geometry. Well, I wasn't particularly interested in geometry—ever. What I was interested in was algebra. I solved the problem, but it didn't give me any joy."

In Bethe's last few years at the *Gymnasium*, he took some

elective physics courses. They were like college freshman physics courses, and included, Bethe recalled, "lots of mechanics." He said, "We used the calculus to calculate trajectories and things like that, and we also did some geometrical optics, which lends itself to mathematical computations. We had some elementary electricity. It was quite clear to me in high school that I wanted to study mathematics or physics—which, I wasn't quite sure. Perhaps a little more physics than mathematics."

Bethe's early years at the *Gymnasium* coincided with the First World War. By the time of the revolution that helped lead to the creation of the Weimar Republic, his father, who was a liberal, had become rector of the university. He took an active part in the negotiations between the university and the city's socialist government, and he ran for the city parliament as a candidate for the Democratic Party, which was the non-socialist left-wing party. "My father went around the district making speeches," Bethe recalled. "He was not elected, and I don't think he had expected to be. But his interest in politics persisted. He had a very liberal point of view but did not want to become a Social Democrat. Even so, he got along well with the Social Democratic city government. I was made much aware of politics, and it was during this period that many of my political attitudes were formed."

Bethe entered the University of Frankfurt in 1924. "Going to the University of Frankfurt made it possible for me to live at home—which was financially necessary and emotionally still good for me," Bethe said. "I took some courses in physics, chemistry, and mathematics. The physics I took in my freshman year was very bad. The professor was really an amateur physicist. Frankfurt, which was a city with great civic pride, had for some time what it called a Physical Society, made up of citizens. When the university was founded, the president of this purely amateur society became the professor of experimental physics. His lectures could not teach me anything new, so I cut most of his classes. Instead, I read a textbook on classical physics by myself. However, there was an associate professor, Walther Gerlach, who was a young man of terrific enthusiasm. In his course in modern physics, he discussed electrons, spectroscopy, atoms, and so on. That was very, very interesting to me. I also took a course in the theory of numbers from Carl Ludwig Siegel"—a distinguished mathematician. "Although I liked the course, and had good personal relations with Siegel, I felt that this was not really what I wanted to work on. Gerlach left after my first year, and was replaced by a spectroscopist named Karl Meissner. He was a nice man, and he told me emphatically that I must not stay in Frankfurt but should go to a place with better theoretical physics. It had become clear to me by this time that I could not do experimental physics. My hands are just no good—I do everything wrong. In the chemistry lab, my lab coat was always in shreds, because I kept getting sulphuric acid on it. Besides, I had realized by then that because of my interest in mathematics I wanted to do theoretical physics. I loved mathematics, but I wanted to apply it to physics. We did have a theoretical physicist at Frankfurt—Erwin Madelung. He was not a very productive physicist, and, though he was well informed, he was scientifically conservative. The course I took with him had to do with classical physics. He never mentioned the quantum theory, and I remained totally unaware of it, even though it was the most exciting physics of the time. In Frankfurt, I studied in sort of a vacuum."

1 / German Beginnings

The quantum theory at this point—1924—was in a state of near-chaos. Niels Bohr, the great Danish physicist, had invented the "old quantum theory" in 1913: by assigning certain allowed (or quantized) orbits for the electron in the hydrogen atom, he was able to account for the observed light spectrum of atomic hydrogen. Bohr derived this result from certain quantum rules, which he had also invented. The rules appeared to be rather ad hoc, however, and as they were extended to the spectra of the heavier atoms, experiments began to contradict them. Furthermore, the theory could not account at all for the relative brightness—the intensities—of the different spectral lines in atoms. Bohr and his colleagues were well aware of the fact that they were dealing not with a consistent theory but with a transitional model of a possible future theory. By 1926, through the work of Bohr, Werner Heisenberg, Erwin Schrödinger, P. A. M. Dirac, Wolfgang Pauli, and others, such a theory had been created. Hence, in Bethe's view Madelung was quite justified in not teaching the old quantum theory to undergraduates; in fact, not to do so was then the standard practice in German universities.

After Bethe had been at Frankfurt for two years, Meissner urged him to leave for Munich. "Meissner not only told me to leave Frankfurt but also told me specifically to go to Sommerfeld," Bethe said. In 1926, Arnold Sommerfeld, the professor of theoretical physics at the University of Munich, was one of the most influential physics teachers in the world, his recent prize pupils having been Wolfgang Pauli and Werner Heisenberg, who by 1923 had both left Munich. Heisenberg went on to win the Nobel Prize in 1932, and Pauli in 1945. Before them, Sommerfeld had had among his pupils Peter Debye and Max von Laue, who also became Nobel Prize winners. Like Bethe, Sommerfeld worked in every area of theoretical physics, and his lectures, which have been published, in several volumes, still form one of the best introductions to many branches of the discipline. "In May of 1926," Bethe recalled, "I presented to Sommerfeld a letter from my father, who had met him by chance somewhere during the war, and a letter from Meissner. I think the letter from Meissner was the one that counted. Sommerfeld said, 'All right, you are very young, but come to my seminar.'"

In those days, at a German university, a professor of Sommerfeld's stature had considerable importance; the physics institute revolved around him and was virtually his private domain. "Sommerfeld had a huge office lined with books, and next to it was an equally large office for his official assistant, who at that time was the well-known theoretical physicist Gregor Wentzel," Bethe said. "And then there was another room of just about the same size, which was simultaneously the library and the abode of everybody else. All the foreign postdoctorals and the German graduate students—eight or ten of us—sat in that room. There was an enormously long table, and we sat at that table as best we could. Later on, when I went back after my doctor's degree, on a fellowship, I got a desk in a separate room. But what a room! Most of it was occupied by a spiral staircase leading to the basement. There was just enough space for a desk and for people to pass when they went up and down the staircase—which they did all day long." In 1926, the first year Bethe was in Munich, Linus Pauling was a postdoctoral fellow, and then came I. I. Rabi and E. U. Condon. "Among the German students at that time was Rudolf Peierls—he is now a British citizen, and is Sir Rudolf Peierls—and he and I became very close friends. We studied together, and we laughed a lot together. Rabi told me later that he and Condon always thought we were laughing at them—which, of course, we were not."

Bethe went on, "Sommerfeld was approachable, but at the same time he was very much the *Geheimrat*—very much the distinguished professor. His dignity was inborn, and was accompanied by a quiet sense of humor. A famous story has it that one of the foreign visitors, in speaking to him, addressed him many times as '*Herr Professor.*' After a few weeks, the visitor was told that Sommerfeld was really *Geheimrat*, whereupon he addressed him, correctly, as '*Herr Geheimrat.*' Sommerfeld is reported to have acknowledged the change by saying, 'You have really learned a lot of German.' Sommerfeld usually gave an advanced course and a seminar. The first course I had with him was in differential equations of physics, which was his specialty. It was an excellent course, and I never missed a class. The seminar met once a week, in the afternoon—I think it started at four and lasted until six or six-thirty. Here Sommerfeld was at his greatest as a teacher. The seminar was where we learned to analyze new material and to enable others to understand it. Sommerfeld would distribute topics or parts of an over-all topic, one to each graduate student and postdoc, and we had to report on them. He himself sat quietly and listened. But if the speaker skipped over a point that Sommerfeld judged necessary, Sommerfeld would interrupt with 'I don't understand,' or, more often, he would ask a very stupid-sounding question, so that the speaker would have to stop and explain, and if he could not explain, then Sommerfeld himself would take over. He did not permit sloppiness.

"Because Sommerfeld was so eminent, he frequently received scientific papers in advance of their public distribution, and so it happened that in 1926 he was sent Schrödinger's papers on wave mechanics as they were being printed. The galleys were distributed to his seminar members, and each of us had to report on one section of them. That was superb. Schrödinger, you will recall, invented wave mechanics—a form of quantum mechanics that is much easier to handle than the one previously known, which was invented by Heisenberg. Nearly all problems in atomic and subatomic physics have since been dealt with by the use of the so-called Schrödinger wave equation. Schrödinger's wave mechanics was one of Sommerfeld's loves, and he followed the papers in detail. Furthermore, he added to them his own polynomial method of solution. Schrödinger, in his papers, did not develop the solutions to his equations but referred the reader to mathematical papers—which were usually hard for physicists to read, because they required a high degree of mathematical knowledge. This habit was rather annoying, and Sommerfeld profoundly disapproved of it. Whenever one of those equations was to come up in the seminar, Sommerfeld's assistant would call in the speaker in advance and say, 'When you come to this point, you do it this way,' and would instruct the speaker in the detailed systematic approach to the solution of the equation as it had been worked out by the *Geheimrat* himself.

"I had the great advantage of not knowing anything about the old quantum theory. For the older generation of physicists, quantum mechanics was difficult to accept, because they had to give up time-honored concepts, like the orbit of a particle. Moreover, the older form of the quantum theory, Bohr's theory of the atom, had led to many contradictions, and had thus got a bad reputation among physicists not completely familiar with it. Although the contradictions were resolved by wave mechanics and its subsequent interpretation and development, the quantum theory was still considered abstruse by many of the older people. To me, who had not gone through all these vagaries, wave mechanics seemed perfectly reasonable from the start, and to the students of today it seems obvious. In 1926, it was convincing to me because it gave the right formulas for the hydrogen atom, and everything seemed to agree with our experiments. The theory was beautiful."

Schrödinger's theory of wave mechanics grew out of the work of the French physicist Prince Louis Victor de Broglie. In 1923, de Broglie became aware that light has a quantum nature as well as the generally recognized wave nature. The energy (E) of a light quantum is related to its wavelength (λ, or lambda) by the Einstein-Planck formula $E = hc/\lambda$, where c is the velocity of light (a hundred and eighty-six thousand miles a second, or 3×10^{10} centimetres per second) and h is Planck's constant (6.625×10^{-27} erg seconds), which is the fundamental constant of the quantum theory. De Broglie proposed that electrons, which up to that time had been thought to be ordinary material particles, had a wave nature besides. He suggested that the wavelength of an electron was given by rewriting the Einstein-Planck formula so that $\lambda = h/p$, where p is the momentum of the electron. The same connection between wavelength and momentum holds for light. De Broglie noticed that if one made this apparently absurd hypothesis the orbits that Bohr had assigned to the electron of a hydrogen atom acquired a new significance. These orbits were characterized by the fact that their circumference was an integer number of de Broglie wavelengths. The de Broglie waves just fitted around the electron orbits, with no overlap. In 1924, Einstein received a copy of de Broglie's doctoral thesis, and felt intuitively that there was something about it that was basically right. He began to examine the consequences. The fact that Einstein was interested brought

the idea to the attention of other physicists, and Schrödinger was led to investigate and then to invent the equation—the Schrödinger equation—that these curious waves
obey.

Unknown to any of these physicists, experiments that,
in effect, confirmed de Broglie's hypothesis had been performed in the United States in 1921. This fact was brought
to light by the physicist Richard Gehrenbeck, writing in
the January 1978 issue of the monthly *Physics Today*. The
article describes experiments that were carried out at the
laboratories of the Western Electric Company, in New
York City, by Clinton Joseph Davisson and Lester Halbert
Germer. Davisson, who initiated the work, had been assigned the job of investigating certain properties of electron
emission from the cathodes used in early vacuum tubes. In
the course of his work, he designed, with the assistance of
Charles Kunsman, who had just received his Ph.D. in physics, an electron gun that enabled him to fire a beam of
energetic electrons against metal grids—in particular, nickel.
Davisson and Kunsman plotted a curve showing that the
number of electrons that scattered from the nickel was
dramatically larger when the electrons rebounded at certain
angles. It was as if the transmission of electrons were magi-
cally enhanced at these special angles. Davisson and Kunsman published their results in 1921 in a brief article in the
journal *Science*. The data were rough, and the experiment-
ers did not connect their observations to related ones that
had been made about X rays a decade earlier in Germany
by Max von Laue and his collaborators. When an X-ray
beam scatters from a crystalline substance, it scatters from
atoms in different planes of the crystal. These scattered
beams can interfere constructively with one another, and
at certain angles there will be maxima, or spots of maximum

intensity, in the so-called diffraction pattern produced by the scattered X rays—the von Laue spots. These diffraction patterns are an essential tool in analyzing the structure of crystals, and their existence demonstrates the wave nature of X rays. In classical physics, waves can interfere with one another, while particles, which is what electrons were considered to be until the mid-nineteen-twenties, cannot. Davisson thought that his results might have something to do with the atomic structure of nickel, but he grew increasingly discouraged about interpreting them precisely. By the end of 1923, he had dropped the project, and Kunsman had left the company.

In 1924, Davisson decided to try once more to understand the pattern in which his electrons were scattered, this time with the assistance of Lester Germer, who had recently returned to Western Electric after an illness. They worked on variations of the original experiment with mixed results until the summer of 1926, when Davisson and his wife decided to visit England. There Davisson went to a meeting of the British Association for the Advancement of Science, at Oxford, and at that meeting, to his astonishment, he heard his and Kunsman's work cited as evidence for the de Broglie waves—which, it turned out, he had never heard of. The wave nature of the electrons was responsible for the diffraction patterns in precise analogy to von Laue's X rays. Davisson spent most of the return voyage from England reading and trying to understand Schrödinger's papers, and he and Germer soon set to work in earnest. By January, they had data that definitively showed the electron's wave nature. G. P. Thomson, the British physicist, working at the University of Aberdeen, in Scotland, had obtained similar results, and in 1937 he and Davisson shared the Nobel Prize in Physics.

I / The Early Years

Beautiful though the results of these experiments were, there remained a dilemma. The X-ray-diffraction theory, applied to electrons, predicted that the angles at which the maxima of the diffraction would occur depended on the wavelength of the electron—or, to turn this notion around, from the diffraction pattern one could compute the wavelength of the electron. But experimental results did not quite fit de Broglie's formula. In 1926, when Bethe went to Sommerfeld for advice about what he might work on, Sommerfeld suggested that he try to account for the discrepancy. Bethe found that if he supposed that while the electrons from Davisson's electron gun were inside the crystal they acquired additional energy—because their interactions with the atoms in the metal accelerated them—they fitted the experimental curves. The value of this additional energy he had to assume arbitrarily so as to obtain a fit. (This phenomenological model had also been proposed, independently of Bethe, by C. H. Eckart, by A. L. Patterson, and by Fritz Zwicky.)

After this simple exercise, Sommerfeld suggested to Bethe, as a problem for his Ph.D. thesis, that he make a detailed theory of the diffraction of electrons by crystals, based on Schrödinger's equation. He suggested that Bethe look for clues in a 1914 paper by Richard Ewald's nephew Paul P. Ewald, also done at Sommerfeld's institute, which dealt with the diffraction of X rays by crystals. So Bethe started out by making a more or less direct translation of Ewald's thesis from X rays to electrons, and found that this worked very well. "But then I became too ambitious and wanted to do it more accurately," he told me. "That did not work at all, because the interaction between electrons and atoms is far too strong. The calculations became quite messy. So my thesis was long and to a large extent messy and unnecessary. It made Pauli say to me when we met for the first time, 'Mr. Bethe, I was very disappointed in your thesis. From Sommerfeld's talk about you, I had expected better of you.' That made me feel just great. But somehow one survived comments of this sort from Pauli."

In 1928, having passed his doctoral examination, Bethe began to look for a job. I asked if Sommerfeld had helped him, and he replied, "He did not. He did nothing. He went on a round-the-world trip. It was the year of his sixtieth birthday, and he did not want it celebrated, so he took a leave and went around the world and returned the following spring. He simply left me to my own devices. Jobs were terribly scarce. The structure of the German universities was hierarchical. Most departments consisted of one professor and in some cases an associate professor, called an 'extraordinary' professor, and then there were some assistants—equivalent to our instructors. There were few of these positions, and the salaries were low—enough for a bachelor but not enough for a family. It seemed quite uncertain whether I could get a job. Many people went into high-school teaching, because the high schools were eager for well-qualified people. In fact, I remember that in my high school practically every teacher had a doctor's degree. This was quite customary, and often necessary for advancement in the German high-school system. In fact, I would say that the job situation was as bad when I got my degree, in 1928, as the American job situation was when I came to the United States, in 1935—during the Depression. There is nothing like it now, as far as physicists are concerned. But one feature of our present situation here is worse—the high schools are generally not willing to take Ph.D.s in physics, or mathematics or English or anything else. They say that these people are overqualified. What a pity, both for the high-school students and for the young people looking for a job! Luckily, near the end of the Depression some of the smaller universities and colleges were happy to take the good young people. They said, 'We know perfectly well that they won't stay very long. They will go to the more famous universities as soon as they get an offer. But if we have them for, say, five years, that will improve the teaching in our university for this time.' " (A recent survey done by the American Physical Society indicates that while most Ph.D.s in physics will find jobs in the mid-nineteen-eighties, less than fifteen percent of the jobs will be in universities.)

Fortunately, soon after Bethe received his degree, he got a teaching offer from Professor Madelung, his former teacher, in Frankfurt, and accepted it. "I was to do research and, together with the assistant in experimental physics, teach the elementary laboratory," Bethe recalled. "We shared the teaching two afternoons a week and got along very well. But as far as research was concerned, Professor Madelung had not changed, and the atmosphere turned out, just as it had two and a half years earlier, to be not especially stimulating. However, I had learned to read the physics journals and to work on my own. I settled down to reading, and learned group theory, an essential mathematical tool for theoretical physicists, and applied it to the behavior of atoms in crystals. Luckily, after half a year I was rescued by Ewald, who asked me to come to Stuttgart as his assistant."

Paul P. Ewald was then professor of theoretical physics at the Technical College of Stuttgart. "He knew about my thesis," Bethe said. "In fact, while I was doing the thesis he had asked me to come to Stuttgart to give a seminar talk. I even remember how he paid me for that seminar. At that time, there were big five-mark pieces, as big as a silver dollar, and he gave me, I think, ten of those pieces. It was the first time anyone had paid me for talking about my own research, and it made me very proud. It was very nice. He liked the talk, and that was lucky, because he had invited me to stay at his home, and I did. He knew that my father had worked at Strasbourg under Richard Ewald, his uncle. I immediately became good friends with Ewald and with Mrs. Ewald, and when his assistant left, in the spring of 1929, he offered me that job, which I readily accepted. The next half year was one of the happiest periods of my young days."

Bethe went on, "I was considered a child of the family. They invited me very often for dinner. They invited me to go on walks with them on Sunday, and if they didn't feel like going themselves they asked me to take the two older children—a boy fourteen and a girl twelve—for walks by myself, which was also very nice. And the girl later became my wife, so I really did become one of the family. The arrangement back in 1929 was a very happy one, and perhaps especially happy for me because my parents had been divorced two years before."

Ewald, who celebrated his ninety-second birthday last January, now lives near the Bethes in Ithaca. On the occasion of his ninetieth birthday, he was honored by the German Physical Society with its Max Planck Medal and by the American Crystallographic Association, at its 1978 spring meeting, with a symposium on his life's work to date. Ewald's dynamic theory provided the basic understanding of the diffraction of X rays in crystals. It was about forty years before modern technology could make crystals close enough to perfect for Ewald's theory to be tested in detail. Nowadays, it is one of the most effective methods of finding imperfections in crystals.

"Ewald ran his department in an open and hospitable

way," Bethe said. "Visitors came from all over the world for long or short stays to give talks and to study under him. One of the talks was by Douglas Hartree, who had just developed the Hartree method." This is a fundamental technique that enables one to deal, in an internally consistent, approximate fashion, with problems that involve many electrons. It is used to compute the properties of heavy atoms, which have large numbers of electrons orbiting the nucleus. "The Hartree method was exactly what I had been waiting for, because I wanted some quantitative way to explain atomic structure," Bethe went on. The next great step forward was taken by the Norwegian physicist Egil Hylleraas, when he applied a variational principle to the helium atom.

A variational principle is a powerful tool for calculating the approximate energy level of an atom. One problem that can be attacked by the variational technique is whether or not certain atomic systems are "bound;" that is, whether they are stable. The helium atom has two electrons orbiting a nucleus with two positive charges, and Hylleraas made the first quantitative calculation of the electrons' energies. It is now a standard example given in quantum-mechanics textbooks.

"Somehow, I had heard that people were interested in the negative hydrogen ion, which is a single proton surrounded by two electrons," Bethe said. "Was it stable? Following Hylleraas's method and using a simple mechanical desk calculator, I soon found out that it was. I did not know then why the stability question was interesting, but now I know that H-minus is important because in the upper layers of the sun, below the photosphere, it is the main absorber of the sun's radiation from the interior— the radiation that does not get out of the sun. [This was first suggested by the astronomer R. Wildt in 1938.] In

1 / *German Beginnings*

Stuttgart, at any rate, I got what I missed so much in Frankfurt—conversations with people who had similar interests. I also did a lot of talking with Ewald himself, and he made a number of useful suggestions in the general area of my thesis—perhaps to improve it, but to no avail. I gave quite a number of seminars. One of my nicest duties came twice a week; namely, to give a course in quantum mechanics to Ewald and all the assistants—both his own and the ones in the Experimental Physics Department. Well, in the midst of this paradise Sommerfeld returned from his trip and found out that I was at Stuttgart. He wrote a postcard to Ewald saying, in effect, 'Bethe is *my* student. I need him for my work in solid-state physics. Send him back immediately.' Ewald and I thought that Sommerfeld had some nerve to do this, but I left it entirely to the two dignified people to fight it out, and of course Sommerfeld won, pulling rank. Though I had been very happy in Stuttgart, I think that scientifically it was good for me to go back to Munich—which I did in the fall of 1929. Sommerfeld offered me a few inducements to sweeten the change. Not only did he provide me with my own little room but he said I could become a *Privatdozent* the following spring, which was unusually early, and he got me a German national fellowship."

That winter, Bethe wrote what he still considers his best paper, even though it was his later work on the energy production in stars that earned him the Nobel Prize. At first sight, the subject matter of the early paper seems almost prosaic, but as it was developed by Bethe and others over the years it encompasses many of the processes that take place in atoms and nuclei when they collide with energetic charged particles. The paper, titled "The Theory of the Passage of Swift Corpuscular Rays Through Matter," appeared in the *Annalen der Physik* in 1930. In 1913, Niels

I / The Early Years

Bohr had presented the classical theory of how charged particles slow down when they pass through matter. Basically, they excite the electrons in the atoms through which they pass, and with each of these "inelastic" collisions the charged particle loses some of its energy. Then, when quantum mechanics was invented, Max Born developed a quantum-theoretic formalism for doing collision theory. This was a triumph for wave mechanics, because the old quantum theory had not been able to deal with collision problems at all. Born's paper was also essential for the correct interpretation of Schrödinger's wave function. Earlier, when Born was the professor of theoretical physics at Göttingen, he had made fundamental contributions to Heisenberg's formulation of quantum mechanics. "But Born's collision theory had been left in a stage where it was rather difficult to do explicit calculations, especially on inelastic collisions," Bethe told me. "I thought I could do that better, and I invented a trick for doing it." Bethe's "trick," which involves a way of rewriting the complicated integrals in the collision formula, is by now standard, and appears in so many textbooks that one almost forgets that it had to be invented by someone. "With that trick, you can do all sorts of things," he added. In his paper, Bethe investigated the role of the electron structure in atoms as it is manifested in these collision processes. In the years since, the energy of the particles passing through matter in experiments has increased, because the particles are being produced by larger and larger accelerators, and the processes that Bethe and others have taken into account have become more and more subtle. Bethe's interest was in basic scientific understanding, but his paper had practical consequences. In modern experiments, physicists have to distinguish many different kinds of particles that may emerge from an experiment, and one means of sorting out the particles is to measure the ionization they produce in a gas. Bethe's theory permits one to calculate this ionization, and thereby distinguish the particles.

Bethe went on, "I submitted this paper to the university in order to become a *Privatdozent*. The process of becoming a *Privatdozent* was a solemn affair. Dressed up in a tuxedo, I had to give my 'inaugural' address in a big auditorium, before an audience of faculty and students. I had to write down a number of theses of my own choosing, which I had to defend against attacks from the audience. Sommerfeld, pro forma, attacked me, as did several of the other professors. There were about fifty people listening. Many of my papers are being put into the Cornell archives now, and while I was sorting them I came across these theses. Some of them were all right, and some of them sound ridiculous now. After that ceremony, I was allowed to give lectures at the university. In the summer of 1930, I gave a course of lectures on collision theory. The other day, I found an old statement from the University of Munich about this. You may recall that at German universities students had to pay for the specific course of lectures they attended. The *Privatdozent* received part of this money, which was known as *Kolleggeld*. I had about twelve students. The statement from the university finance office consisted of a long sheet that started out with what the students had paid, then listed what the university would keep—the taxes and seven other items that were being subtracted. I ended up with fifty marks for a term's work." Fifty marks was then twelve dollars.

Bethe's first vague glimmering of the growing change in political attitudes in Germany came in 1928. He told me,

I / The Early Years

"I wasn't at that time aware of any trouble brewing. Of course, I read the newspapers, but I read only what seemed important to me then. Economic developments, international relations—things like that. I found talking to my fellow-students about politics to be essentially impossible. I found them to be ultra-conservative and unrealistically nationalistic. Not so much the ones in theoretical physics as the ones in other fields. Their talk seemed absolutely crazy to me. They were forever talking about Imperial Germany coming back and about the horrible injustice of the Treaty of Versailles. I agreed that the Treaty of Versailles was quite nasty to Germany, but it was a fact, and I thought that Germany should try its best to live within this framework. Indeed, it had been doing very well from 1925 to 1928. There were a few of the physics students who were in the Nazi movement, but it was not until the 1930 elections to the Reichstag, when the Nazis got something like a hundred out of five hundred delegates—a jump from ten or twenty—that I felt that things might easily go wrong."

Bethe spent part of the years 1930 and 1931 outside Germany. He had been awarded a Rockefeller Foundation fellowship, which he used to visit Cambridge University and then Rome, where he worked at the University of Rome with Enrico Fermi. "Sommerfeld suggested that I divide the time between two countries," Bethe said. "First, he suggested that I go to England and the United States. He felt that I should go to Davisson, in New York. Davisson, for some reason, wasn't interested, and in any case, as it turned out, it would have been a mistake. So I went to Rome instead, also at Sommerfeld's suggestion. England was a revelation to me—I found that the English had a much healthier attitude toward life than the Germans. You could talk to them about politics, philosophy, or anything else in a reasonable way. They didn't look for mysterious origins somewhere. The mystical element in the life philosophy of many Germans had always repelled me, and still does. In England, everything was clear and simple. I was happy. I lived in a boarding house that served the worst food you can imagine, but I was frequently invited to the colleges for dinner, and that was always a treat. There was a lot of good talk in college after dinner. There were delightful old men, learning to fly at the age of sixty. They and the rest were very sensible about politics, and they took life pretty well the way it came. England at that time was a happy country in comparison to Germany—quite prosperous and with a much wider horizon."

I asked Bethe if during this time he had encountered P. A. M. Dirac, who later assumed the Lucasian Professorship of Mathematics at Cambridge—a professorship that had once been held by Isaac Newton.

"Dirac gave a course in the quantum theory in which he read the material word for word from his book," Bethe said. "Somebody once asked him why he did that, and he said, 'When I wrote the book, I thought very hard about how to formulate it, and there is no better way.' Early in my stay, I attended some of Dirac's lectures, along with another German postdoc. He found it useful to attend because he learned how the words in Dirac's book were pronounced. I had learned English, and I didn't find that sufficient reason to listen to what I could read, so I went only two or three times and then stopped."

After his stay in Cambridge, Bethe went to Fermi in Rome. Fermi was just thirty, but even then he was an internationally known physicist. "He was a professor, which I was very far from being, and he was already a member of a special academy in Rome that Mussolini had created," Bethe said. "Because of this, he had the title Excellency, a higher title than Sommerfeld's *Geheimrat*. But what a difference! Where Sommerfeld had been approachable but still always the dignitary, Fermi did not seem to have the word 'formality' in his vocabulary. He was one of the least stuffy people I have ever met. You could go to him anytime, and it was like two graduate students talking to each other. Let me tell you just one anecdote. Fermi used to wear a leather jacket, and he always drove his own car. One day, he encountered a roadblock right in front of his institute. He leaned out of the window and said to the policeman, 'I am His Excellency Enrico Fermi's chauffeur' —which, of course, got him waved on, whereas a statement that he was His Excellency Enrico Fermi himself would not have been believed. Fermi seemed to me at the time like the bright Italian sunshine. Clarity appeared wherever his mind took hold. I was tremendously impressed by his facility with physics—by his way of looking at a problem. Somebody would come to him and say, 'I don't know how to solve such-and-such a problem,' and Fermi would say, 'All right, let's think. Perhaps we could do it this way.' And, talking aloud about his own thinking process, he would develop the general theory of this particular problem. Once he had solved a problem, it was obvious that this was the way to do it. In the simplest, most straightforward manner, you could then proceed to act on the knowledge gained from Fermi's analysis. Discussions ranged over every aspect of physics. For all these reasons, Fermi was a magnet for Italian physicists, who, no matter where they might be teaching or studying, spent a good deal of time in Rome. I met, among others, Emilio Segrè, Franco Rasetti, Edoardo Amaldi, Giulio Racah, and Bruno Rossi, all of whom became prominent later on. From Fermi I learned lightness of approach; that is, to look at things qualitatively first and understand the problem physically before putting a lot of formulas on paper. Sommerfeld never could have done that and never would have. Sommerfeld's method was to start out by inserting the data of a problem into an appropriate mathematical equation and solving the equation quantitatively according to the strictest mathematical formalism for those specific data, and finally he would interpret the results for their physical significance. Under his tutelage, you never looked at the problem first with a view to finding the easiest way to solve it. It was from Fermi that I learned to do this. Fermi was as much an experimenter as a theorist, and the mathematical solution was for him more a confirmation of his understanding of a problem than the basis for it. Both approaches have their uses and advantages. For me, it was very important to learn both. Fermi and I wrote a paper comparing three methods of treating the relativistic electron-electron interaction—unifying electro-magnetic quantum theory with relativity. The research took two days. Then he said, 'Well, now we have solved it, now we will write a paper.' So on the third day he himself sat down at the typewriter—there was no secretary in the institute. His procedure was to state a sentence in German—he spoke excellent German, while I spoke hardly any Italian—and I would either approve it or modify it. When we came to an equation, we would agree on it, and I would write it down in longhand. That was the paper. It came to ten printed pages in the *Zeitschrift für Physik*. It was a nice paper, and even though Fermi did by far the larger part of it, it had my name on it along with his. I felt very happy about that, and I learned a lot from it. It taught me how to write a scientific paper simply and clearly. My stay in Rome came to an end much too soon."

In 1931, Bethe returned to Munich. "The Depression

came," Bethe said. "In 1930, it was still not very noticeable, but by 1931 there was a deep depression. There was terrific unemployment all over Germany. I think twenty percent of the labor force was unemployed, and in certain regions things were even worse. There was a lot of misery. At one point, in the summer of 1931, the banks were closed. And some banks failed, among them two of the biggest banks. Fortunately, my parents' money was not in either of those. But the accounts in all banks were blocked for a while, so you had to live on promises. I was apprehensive, fearing that the situation would lead to catastrophe, but I certainly did not anticipate that the Nazis might take over the government. I thought that maybe they would get into the government, but I did not dream that anything would happen that would force me to leave the country. For me, the years 1931 and 1932 were a very good working period. Because of my newly acquired English, Sommerfeld turned over to me all his English and American postdocs. One of the American postdocs was Lloyd Smith, from Cornell. I gave him a nice problem involving the Hartree method. A few years later, when I had to leave Germany, he suggested to his department chairman at Cornell, where he had become a professor in the meantime, that I be asked to come there. I accepted, of course, and, as you know, have been there ever since."

In 1932, Bethe, in collaboration with Sommerfeld, wrote one of his three great review articles. It was published in 1933 in the *Handbuch der Physik*, under the title "Elektronen-theorie der Metalle," and contained the basis for the modern solid-state theory of metals. He also paid a second visit to Fermi in Rome. "During this time, the political situation in Germany was rapidly becoming worse," Bethe told me. "For me personally, things were still all right. Sometime in the summer of 1932, I got an offer from Tübingen, an old and very good university in Württemberg. It was for a sort of assistant professorship in theoretical physics, and I went there in November of 1932. Hans Geiger"—the inventor of the Geiger counter, for measuring radioactivity —"was the professor of experimental physics. He was interested in my quantum-mechanics course, and came to it regularly. I gave that course for advanced students and for, essentially, the entire experimental-physics faculty. I also gave a course in electrodynamics. I had a good time scientifically in Tübingen. Gieger explained his experiments to me, and in other ways made a lot of me, so all seemed to be well on the personal level. However, the general atmosphere in Tübingen had become very bad. Many students wore the brown shirts and swastika armbands of the National Socialist organization. Some of them were in my classes. It was clear from the way people talked, from the way students talked—perhaps not the majority, but the most vocal of them—that they were confirmed Nazis. This showed afterward, on the thirtieth of January, when Hitler was named Chancellor. The Nazis had a tremendous torch parade through the city. It was quite clear where Tübingen's heart was."

I asked Bethe whether the wearing of armbands by the students in class was something new.

"It was indeed," Bethe replied. "I had never seen it in the classroom in Munich, either in Sommerfeld's institute or in the experimental institute. But suddenly it was inescapable. Also, it was evident that the German economy wasn't getting any better. Brüning"—Heinrich Brüning had been selected by the German President, Field Marshal von Hindenburg, to head a coalition government in 1930—"followed a policy of deflation, which increased unemployment. He was succeeded by Franz von Papen, then by Kurt von Schleicher, who gave way to Hitler. Hindenburg was so old that he did not understand what was happening. It was clear that catastrophe was coming—and it came. But even after the Nazis began to govern Germany, I still did not think I would have to leave. I remember that during February of 1933 I went to the Ewalds, in Stuttgart, for some kind of festivity. Stuttgart was only an hour's bus ride from Tübingen. At that party, I talked really quite foolishly. I was still optimistic, whereas Ewald was depressed and sure that things would be very, very bad. I simply did not think that anybody could do all the things Hitler said in 'Mein Kampf' he was going to do. It was inconceivable."

The Reichstag fire occurred on February 27, 1933, and soon after that Hitler took over Germany. On April 4, 1933, the first racial laws were promulgated. Jews were declared unfit for government service, and since the universities were run by the state, this decree applied to all Jews connected to them. "I had been to Austria on a beautiful ski trip," Bethe recalled. "Just a day or two before I returned, there was a boycott of Jewish stores—on the first of April. Then there were the racial laws, and I was not sure how strictly they would be applied. But it was clear that according to the laws I could not hold a university position, because two of my grandparents were Jewish. The first I heard about this directly was when one of my two Ph.D. students in Tübingen wrote me a letter saying, 'I read in the papers that you have been dismissed. What shall I do? Tell me what shall I do?' What should *he* do? I had not heard of my dismissal, but it had been published in the papers. I asked him for the clipping, and he sent it to me. It turned out that there were only two of us whom they had been able to dismiss without difficulty. Then I wrote to Geiger, who had been so friendly to me. He wrote back a completely cold letter saying that with the changed situation it would be necessary to dispense with my further services—period. There was no kind word, no regret—nothing. Then, a few days later, I got a letter from the Württemberg Ministry of Cultural Affairs which said that I was dismissed in accordance with the law but that my salary would be paid for April—which was the month in which I was dismissed—and that was that. So, of course, I wrote to Sommerfeld crying for help, and Sommerfeld immediately replied, 'You are most welcome here. I will have your fellowship again for you. Just come back.' "

"Sommerfeld must have been a great man," I observed.

"He *was* a great man," Bethe replied. "Not only did he do that for me but he spent most of the summer term of 1933 finding jobs for the various people with Jewish ancestors who were in any way connected with him. He must have found jobs then for at least half a dozen people. He went out of his way to write letters to everybody he knew —and he knew almost everybody—trying to place the Jewish, half-Jewish, or quarter-Jewish physicists somewhere. Mostly in England. Maybe one or two in France. He had no fear. He was an old man. He was a man of great reputation. He did not think that anybody would do anything to him—and, indeed, nobody did. He was allowed to serve out his term until retirement. The only unpleasant thing he suffered was that when he retired he had no influence on the choice of his successor. He wanted Werner Heisenberg to be his successor—the best choice possible—and Heisenberg wanted to come. Not only had he grown up in Munich but he liked Sommerfeld very much, and Munich, next to Berlin, was the university with the greatest prestige. But the government found Heisenberg not acceptable—not sufficiently Nazi—so he was rejected. Instead, they appointed a man who had been, I think, an assistant to Johannes Stark"—an early and eager Nazi convert—"and had absolutely no idea of theoretical physics. None. I believe he had never published a paper apart from his thesis. But he was a Nazi with a very low Party number, and so he was put in. After that, I think, Sommerfeld did not enter the institute again until after the war. He took all his books home and worked at home—paid no further attention to the university."

Sommerfeld, who died in Munich on April 26, 1951, retained an active interest in physics until the end of his life. In 1948, when Bethe paid his first visit to Germany after the war, he went to see Sommerfeld, and although Sommerfeld was in his eightieth year and nearly deaf, he was eager to learn about the latest results of research. As Sommerfeld's case suggests, the Nazis seemed to have a policy of more or less ignoring the activities of the older scientists but crushing any dissent by younger people. Bethe now thinks that if the Nazis had attacked the older, distinguished men, they would have encountered some opposition. The rapid deterioration of science that took place in Germany after the passage of the racial laws has been documented in a recent book, *Scientists Under Hitler*, by the historian Alan D. Beyerchen. Among those scientists who left the country, Beyerchen points out, Bethe was one of nineteen who had won the Nobel Prize or would eventually win it. For those who remained, doing science had an unreal quality. Bethe gave me a remarkable illustration of this unreality. The helium atom has been found to have two completely separate sets of spectral lines, known as orthohelium and parahelium. These distinct systems can be traced back to the quantum states of the two electrons that orbit the helium nucleus. One of Pauli's great discoveries in quantum mechanics is the so-called exclusion principle, which limits the states that two identical particles like the helium electrons can occupy. In particular, the lowest energy state of parahelium—the "ground" state—does not, according to quantum mechanics, have any counterpart in orthohelium. A few weeks after the racial laws were passed, Stark was appointed president of the German equivalent of the Bureau of Standards. "One of the people on the staff was a very good spectroscopist named Kopfermann," Bethe said. "Stark considered himself a spectroscopist, too, and told his staff, 'We had better look for the ground state of orthohelium.' Kopfermann knew, of course, that this state doesn't exist, but he also knew that Stark didn't believe in quantum mechanics—he characterized it as a 'Jewish invention'—so he couldn't tell Stark directly that, according to this theory, that state doesn't exist. So Kopfermann looked off into the air and said, 'Herr President, I have a hunch that that state doesn't exist.' Hunches were considered to be fine, and so when Stark and all his collaborators couldn't find the state, Kopfermann became a great man, because he had the right German feeling for how to do physics."

In 1933, although Bethe was relatively secure under Sommerfeld's wing, it had become clear to him that he would have to leave Germany soon. "In 1933, there were already people being sent to concentration camps," he said. "Dachau was very close to Munich, and people told hair-raising stories about the treatment of the prisoners. At that time, there was one Nazi student in Sommerfeld's institute, and there was one Communist, and then there was me. The Communist and I used to talk to each other—exchange political stories and stories about the concentration camp. Luckily, after a short time the factotum of the institute, a Jack-of-all-trades but primarily a machinist, came to us and said, 'Now, look, boys, what you are doing is dangerous. Stop talking! There is the Nazi, listening, and any day he may denounce you.' Although I gave a lecture course in Munich without any disturbance, I was also supposed to give a big colloquium—a joint experimental and theoretical colloquium—about the neutron, which had just been discovered. But the day before it was scheduled I was told that I must not give it, because the students would make demonstrations—very violent demonstrations—if I did."

At this time, fortunately, Bethe received an offer of a temporary lectureship at the University of Manchester, and he accepted it at once. "There was a very slight question in my father's mind about my leaving Germany," Bethe said. "He wrote asking me whether I would not rather take a position in industry—which I could have held, since it would not have been a state position. But he didn't take that idea very seriously. My Greek Uncle, on the other hand, was all against my leaving. I tried only halfheartedly to explain it to him. He wouldn't have agreed, no matter what I said—and nothing he said persuaded me. My mother was quite upset. She was terribly attached to me, especially after the divorce. It was financially impossible at that time for her to emigrate. She would have been allowed to take out about six thousand dollars, and she could not have lived on that. She was being paid alimony by my father, which could not have been paid abroad, so leaving was out of the question for her.

"Also, it did not seem dangerous at that time for her to stay. I went back to Germany from England and the United States many times to see her, even in 1938, when

I had considerable misgivings—I was not sure whether I would ever get out again. I tried in letters to make it clear to her that it would be much nicer for us to meet in Switzerland that time, but she didn't understand. So I had to go back into Germany. On this occasion, I also saw my father, with his new family. Then my mother and I left for Switzerland. At the frontier, nobody said anything, even though I was of military age and had a German passport. I had American residency by then, but that did not change my German citizenship. During our time together in Switzerland, my mother and I had several visitors who were in search of jobs in America. Their tales, as much as my urging, made my mother realize that she, too, should consider emigration. I tried to persuade her to stay in Switzerland until I could get her here, but she returned to Germany. In the fall of 1938, there were the real pogroms. She herself was not arrested, but one of her cousins was. My mother's passport was stamped with the information that she was Jewish and, as happened to most Jewish women, the name Sarah was added to her name. She had to wear the yellow star on the outside of her clothing whenever she went out of the house. All this finally upset her sufficiently so that she really prepared for emigration. She was very lucky. Because she had been born in Strasbourg, she was able to get her immigration visa on the French quota, which had room. The German quota was by then full. She left Germany to come to America in June of 1939, just before the war."

In addition to the article that Bethe wrote with Sommerfeld on the solid-state theory of metals, he had written a review article on quantum-mechanical systems involving one and two electrons. In 1957, it was translated and brought up to date, with the collaboration of the Cornell physicist E. E. Salpeter, under the title "Quantum Mechanics of One- and Two-Electron Atoms." It remains the basic reference on this subject. "When I left Germany for Manchester," Bethe continued, "I took with me about three thousand dollars—the proceeds of my two long articles in the *Handbuch der Physik*. In 1933, there was no difficulty in taking this money out of Germany. In fact, I could have taken twice as much if I had had it. I simply went to the regional internal-revenue office and stated my case, and the people there immediately put their signature to it. My future wife, who emigrated three years later, was allowed to take out ten marks—then four dollars."

Chapter 2

America: The First Years

FOR some five years before Bethe left Germany, he and Peierls had exchanged letters. Professor Peierls recently told me that Bethe used to attach serial numbers to his own letters. Peierls saved Bethe's letters and has now deposited them in the Bodleian Library, at Oxford, the university from which he recently retired as the chairman of the Theoretical Physics Department. On a 1930 trip to Russia, Peierls had fallen in love with a young Russian physics student, Genia Kannegiesser, and returned the following year to marry her. She had come with him to Manchester, where he had a position at the university. Even at twenty-five, Genia Peierls was, in Bethe's words, "a formidable woman, generous to a fault, immensely energetic, and used to taking command." He added, "She has remained that way, and generations of physicists have come under her tutorial wing." Bethe was the first of a long line of physicists who lived with the Peierls. "She took my education in hand," Bethe remarked. "I learned quite a lot from her about worldly behavior and not being afraid of people. Physicists were no problem, but I was afraid of most other people. Living with Rudi and Genia was a happy arrangement in every respect. Rudi and I worked together. He had just become interested in studying the atomic nucleus, and I joined him in that." For her part, Genia Peierls recalls Bethe's extraordinary dedication to his work. On one occasion she noticed that he had just thrown away two hundred pages of incomplete calculations. When she asked him about it he remarked cheerfully, as she remembers it, that he had made a mistake of a minus sign somewhere and was about to start over again from the beginning.

James Chadwick, working at Cambridge, had discovered the neutron in 1932, and now physicists were beginning to explore the applications of quantum mechanics to nuclei. Peierls and Bethe made frequent visits to Cambridge, and during one of them they learned that Chadwick and Maurice Goldhaber, now of the Brookhaven National Laboratory, on Long Island, were in the process of splitting the nucleus of heavy hydrogen, or deuteron, by irradiating it with energetic light quanta—gamma rays. Chadwick told Bethe and Peierls that in his view no one would be able to come up with a theory of the process. "So Rudi and I went home together and developed the theory and wrote what I still think is a nice paper," Bethe said. "Unfortunately, I had no prospect of staying in Manchester, since I was only replacing someone who was on a year's leave of absence. But my old friend Mott"—now Sir Nevill Mott, who shared the 1977 Nobel Prize in Physics with John H.

Van Vleck, of Harvard, and Phillip W. Anderson, of the Bell Laboratories and Princeton—"whom I had known from my previous visit to England, was working at Bristol. I gave a talk there, and rather wistfully intimated that I would love to come to Bristol. He took the hint and, a few weeks later, offered me a fellowship at Bristol for a year, with the chance that it might be renewed. But in the summer of 1934 I got a cable, out of the blue, from Cornell offering me an acting assistant professorship, with the prospect that it might be made into something permanent."

Bethe knew next to nothing about Cornell when he accepted the job, and what he heard about it during the next few months hardly reassured him. "I met a physicist who had been there. He said, 'Don't go to that place. It is a terrible place. It is so straitlaced that you have to go to church every Sunday. You won't like it at all.' I accepted anyway, and when I was offered a salary of three thousand dollars a year I considered myself immensely rich. I came in early February of 1935. What I found was a department full of ambition. A new chairman, R. C. Gibbs, had just been selected, and he explained to me that the department was changing from one in which research was done to provide thesis topics for graduate students to one in which graduate students could participate in ongoing research. Not everyone agreed with this new emphasis on research, and there was some disagreement on which fields to expand into. It was the progressives versus the conservatives. The progressives had won the fight and now had the backing of the administration. My appointment—I was a theoretical nuclear man, and a foreigner to boot—was one of the signs of change. The year before, it had been decided to build a cyclotron—the first one to be built outside of Berkeley—and Gibbs had brought in M. S. Livingston for this purpose, because Livingston had assisted E. O. Lawrence during the building of the original cyclotron, in 1930, and is generally credited with having made it actually run after Lawrence had the idea for it. The third man to be appointed in nuclear physics was R. F. Bacher. The Cornell Physics Department was a very friendly one, and I immediately became part of it. I felt perfectly at home, and was glad I had exchanged England for America. Though I had had an excellent time with my colleagues and my friends in England, it was clear there that I was a foreigner and would remain a foreigner. In America, people made me feel at once that I was going to be an American—that maybe I was one already. In fact, after going home for the summer to see my mother I felt that Germany was much stranger than America—that it was a weird country."

Bethe continued, "I found my colleagues at Cornell terribly eager to learn, but not very knowledgeable. The courses that I gave to the graduate students were a lot of fun, but on the whole the students didn't have as much background as I had expected. Livingston, who had done a lot of nuclear physics before, had a big card file of all the papers that had been written on nuclear physics. Imagine having that now! But he didn't really understand many of the basic ideas. So I explained them to him, and then I explained them to Lloyd Smith, and then I was invited around the country and explained some more nuclear physics here and there. Finally, I decided that it would really be much easier if I wrote it all down. That was the basis of my articles on nuclear physics in *Reviews of Modern Physics*. I wrote essentially everything I knew in those articles."

The first of the articles was written with Bacher and was published in 1936. Many years later, Bacher recalled, "Bethe wrote these articles seated under a very dim light in

Rockefeller Hall at Cornell, a large pile of blank paper on his right and a pile of completed manuscript on his left. Bethe always wrote in ink, with some, but not very many, corrections, even to complicated calculations. He was and is indefatigable, and worked regularly from midmorning till late at night—but would always stop cheerfully to answer questions."

The second article, which Bethe wrote by himself, appeared in 1937, along with the third, written in collaboration with Livingston. "I talked a lot with Livingston about his experiments on the then new Cornell cyclotron," Bethe told me. "It cost eight hundred dollars and was the second-smallest working cyclotron ever built. We wanted to build a bigger one, and one of the things I did in those days was to design a cyclotron that would use the minimum amount of iron. Iron was expensive. That was the first purely engineering calculation I did in my life."

In the spring of 1938, Bethe went to Washington to attend a meeting on astrophysics sponsored by the Carnegie Institution's Department of Terrestrial Magnetism. The meeting—a small one by today's standards, involving only thirty-four people—had been arranged by two George Washington University physicists, George Gamow and Edward Teller. Astrophysics up to that time had developed separately from theoretical physics. Though the astrophysicists had been able to calculate the interior structure of a star when they knew only the surface temperature, the size, and the mass—a tremendous achievement—they did not know the source of a star's energy. They did suspect that reactions among atomic nuclei probably played a role. In the light of that suspicion, Gamow and Teller became convinced that the problem was ripe for theoretical physicists, and they and some of their students were working on it.

I / The Early Years

The conference had been organized so that other physicists could learn the basic facts from the astrophysicists and get into the subject. Gamow, who had a mischievous sense of humor and a prodigious imagination, claimed—and this claim is still repeated in some books as serious history—that on the train ride back to Cornell afterward Bethe invented the carbon cycle that accounts for the energy production in stars hotter than the sun. Gamow also added Bethe's name to a paper he had written with a collaborator, Ralph Alpher, in 1948, so that the author list would read "Alpher, Bethe, and Gamow." Commenting on this bit of mischief in an article in Bethe's "birthday book" Gamow noted, "In writing up the preliminary communication of this work I was unhappy that the letter β was missing between α and γ. Thus, sending the manuscript for publication in *Physical Review* I put the name of Hans Bethe (in absentia) between our names. This was planned as a surprise to Hans when he would unexpectedly find his name as coauthor, and I was sure that, being my old friend, and having a good sense of humor he would not mind.

"What I did not know," Gamow continues, "was that at that time he was one of the reviewers for *Physical Review* and that the manuscript was sent to him for evaluation. But he did not make any changes in it except to strike out the words "in absentia" after his name. . . ." Indeed, Bethe himself has something of a fondness for jokes of this kind. For example, a few years earlier, in 1936, in one of his review articles he inserted several references to a non-existent paper by Bohr. The paper was given the nominal publication date of 1939 since Bethe felt that Bohr, who was notorious about such things, would take at least three years to write up the work, which, in 1936, Bethe knew that Bohr had already completed.

Bethe actually began working on his carbon-cycle theory after he returned to Cornell and, as he recalls it, the theory took him about six weeks to complete. By that time, no one who was working in astrophysics had much doubt that the energy emitted by the sun and other stars was due to nuclear fusion. In fusion reactions, two light nuclei collide and "fuse"—form a new nucleus—and the energy released is mainly in the form of gamma rays (γ). Relatively elusive particles called neutrinos are also emitted. There is a loss of mass, the mass being converted into radiant energy according to Einstein's equation $E = mc^2$.

The question remaining was what fused into what in a star like the sun. It was known that most of the mass of the sun is made up of hydrogen and helium. (About two percent of the mass is in heavier elements—carbon, nitrogen, and oxygen.) Hence, the energy-production mechanism had to make use primarily of hydrogen and helium nuclei. The German physicist C. F. von Weizsäcker had proposed a year earlier that the basic reaction must be the fusion of two hydrogen protons. This reaction produces a deuteron, which consists of a proton and a neutron bound together, a positron, and a neutrino. Symbolically:

$$P + P \rightarrow D + e^+ + \nu$$

where P stands for proton, D for deuteron, e^+ for positron, and ν for neutrino. This reaction does not liberate much energy. But the newly formed deuteron starts a chain of reactions, the net result of which is that hydrogen is transformed into helium, with the release of a large amount of energy. This is real alchemy: we need the sun's energy a lot more than we need gold.

Von Weizsäcker had suggested the basic P-P fusion reaction, but he had not calculated the rate to see if it agreed with the actual rate of energy production in the sun. The sun radiates energy at a rate of 3.86×10^{33} ergs per second (or, equivalently, about 3.86×10^{23} kilowatts), and any valid theory must reproduce this rate. C. L. Critchfield, who was a student of Gamow and Teller, decided to calculate the rate of the *P-P* fusion reaction. To do so, Critchfield needed to know, among other things, the quantum-mechanical intricacies of the deuteron, and he turned to Bethe for help. "By the time of the Washington conference, we had our calculation done," Bethe told me. "We knew that it fitted the energy production of the sun. But the *P-P* fusion reaction did not seem to fit the bigger stars. So I said to myself, 'Well, maybe there is something else for these bigger stars.' I went through the periodic table step by step and looked at the various nuclei that could react with protons. Nothing seemed to work, and I was almost ready to give up. But when I tried carbon, it worked. So, you see, this was a discovery by persistence, and not by brains. Once I had discovered the carbon cycle, I was able to do the detailed calculations rather easily, since I knew from my review articles how nuclear reactions vary with temperature, and so on."

The central temperature of a star is a crucial factor in dictating which of the nuclear reactions—*P-P* or carbon cycle—is responsible for energy production. In the interior of the sun, where the fusion reactions take place, the temperature is now estimated to be about fourteen million degrees Kelvin. (Zero degrees Kelvin is –459.69 degrees Fahrenheit.) At very high temperatures, all the electrons are stripped off the atoms. An atom has a positively charged nucleus, and surrounding this, at lesser temperatures, is a cloud of electrons—negatively charged particles.

These two types of charge normally make the atom as a whole electrically neutral. But when the atoms are heated up they collide, and as the temperature continues to increase, these collisions get more violent, until the electrons are knocked off the nucleus. At enormous stellar temperatures, the electrons never get a chance to regain their place, and so at the center of a star matter exists in its plasma state—as a gas of free electrons and free, positively charged nuclei. The fusion takes place among these positively charged nuclei. Now, two like charges will repel each other, so the repulsion of the charges must be overcome if fusion is to occur. According to classical physics, this repulsion will never be overcome, since such an action would lead to a violation of the conservation of energy. But quantum physics is more flexible: many processes that cannot happen according to classical physics can happen, but with a small probability. In this instance, the theory determines the probability, which depends strongly on the central temperature of a star.

The central temperature is not easy to arrive at experimentally. What we see of a star like the sun is the light coming from the surface, so we can directly measure the surface temperature by analyzing this light. In the case of the sun, the surface temperature is fifty-seven hundred degrees K. At the time of the Washington meeting that Bethe attended in 1938, Sir Arthur Eddington had estimated the central temperature of the sun to be forty million degrees. At such a temperature, however, nuclear reaction proceeds too quickly; that is, the rate gives a much larger energy production than is observed. But at the Washington meeting the Danish astronomer Bengt Strömgren pointed out that if the sun contained a good deal of hydrogen the central temperature could be much lower than Eddington had calculated. He thought that it might be as low as twenty million degrees. At this temperature, the nuclear reactions do proceed at the right rate for the observed energy production, and, Bethe said, "that sounded better for our reaction probabilities." At twenty million degrees, the Bethe carbon cycle is the dominant energy process, and for a while after Bethe invented it he thought that it might account for the energy production in all the stars. But in the next few years it became apparent that even Strömgren's estimate was too high for the sun's temperature—that its temperature was closer to fourteen million degrees, the currently accepted value. At this temperature, the von Weizsäcker-Bethe-Critichfield process is the dominant energy-production mechanism. The literature on stellar-energy production dating from this time is necessarily ambiguous, because no one knew quite what the temperatures were. If one reads Bethe's seminal paper, one can easily get the idea that the energy production in all the stars comes from the carbon cycle. A little later in the development of the subject, he changed his mind, and now we know that the P-P calculations he and Critchfield presented in 1938 really do fit the sun and explain solar-energy production. The carbon cycle is relevant for hotter and more massive stars, like Sirius and Cygnus Y.

The Bethe carbon cycle was a six-step process to convert hydrogen into helium, releasing about the same large amount of energy as the conversion of hydrogen into helium by the process that starts with the P-P reaction. In the carbon cycle, the carbon acts as a catalyst. It is not destroyed, and that is why Bethe's sequence of reactions is referred to as a cycle. In the sun, the carbon cycle is a relatively unimportant mechanism for energy production, but it takes over in the stars whose central temperature is greater than about eighteen million degrees. The six steps involve nitrogen (N) and oxygen (O), which are manufactured as the cycle proceeds, and for this reason it is sometimes referred to as the *C-N-O* cycle. The first five steps are these:

$$C^{12} + P \rightarrow N^{13} + \gamma$$
$$N^{13} \rightarrow C^{13} + e^+ + \nu$$
$$C^{13} + P \rightarrow N^{14} + \gamma$$
$$N^{14} + P \rightarrow O^{15} + \gamma$$
$$O^{15} \rightarrow N^{15} + e^+ + \nu$$

And, finally:

$$N^{15} + P \rightarrow C^{12} + He^4$$

Working out the details was what took Bethe six weeks. "The paper was finished in the summer of 1938," Bethe told me. "I sent it to the *Physical Review*. But I had a graduate student named Bob Marshak. He had been sent to me by Rabi in 1937, in the same way that I was sent to Sommerfeld. We got along together very well, and he was very much interested in astrophysics. He followed my calculations closely, and one day he said, 'Did you know that the New York Academy of Sciences has a prize for the best paper on energy production in stars? It's five hundred dollars. Why don't you submit your paper? But it must not have been published.' So I asked the *Physical Review* to return the paper to me, and I promised Marshak a finder's fee of ten per cent. I got the prize, and he got the fifty dollars. I used part of the prize to help my mother emigrate. The Nazis were quite willing to let my mother out, but they wanted two hundred and fifty dollars, in dollars, to release her furniture. Part of the prize money went to liberate my mother's furniture. Marshak also knew

I / The Early Years

about a W.P.A. project in New York where a group under the physicist Arnold Lowan did mathematical computation. He suggested that we ask for help in calculating the internal distribution of temperature and density in the sun. And this became the first modern determination of the temperature in a star." Subsequently, the carbon-cycle paper was duly published by the *Physical Review*, which is the standard American physics journal. As for Robert Marshak, he has had a distinguished career in physics and was until recently the president of the City College of New York.

There is a fascinating scientific epilogue to this tale. To understand it we must expand somewhat on the solar *P-P* fusion process. As we have indicated, the initial fusion reaction—the one whose probability Bethe computed—is:

$$P + P \rightarrow D + e^+ + \nu$$

But once formed the deuteron (*D*) rapidly fuses with another proton to make a light isotope of helium (He^3). Symbolically:

$$D + P \rightarrow He^3 + \gamma$$

Now the heliums can collide and there are two possibilities:

$$He^3 + He^3 \rightarrow He^4 + P + P$$
$$\text{or}$$
$$He^3 + He^4 \rightarrow Be^7 + \gamma$$

Here Be^7 stands for beryllium. But now the beryllium can collide and an isotope of Boron (B^8) can be manufactured:

$$Be^7 + P \rightarrow B^8 + \gamma$$

(It might seem, by the way, that this can continue indefinitely, producing all the elements in the periodic table. As it turns out, this does not work, and the heavy elements, heavier than iron, are produced in violent processes involving the collapse of old stars, with the resultant production of nova or supernova explosions.) Boron now decays in the process:

$$B^8 \rightarrow He^4 + He^4 + e^+ + \nu$$

in which one of the final products is a characteristic neutrino of exceptionally high energy: 10 MeV.

All neutrinos interact very weakly with matter, and these solar neutrinos escape from the sun in about three seconds. It takes the more strongly interacting gamma rays about a million years to get from the interior to the surface of the sun. But these high-energy neutrinos should be detectable here on earth. The basic identifying technique was worked out by the Brookhaven physicist Raymond Davis Jr., who has been trying to detect these neutrinos since 1968. Davis noticed that if these high-energy neutrinos impinged on chlorine they could convert the chlorine into argon by the process:

$$\nu + Cl^{37} \rightarrow Ar^{37} + e^-$$

Chlorine is a good target choice since it can be stored, in large quantities, in liquids like carbon tetrachloride, a commonly used cleaning fluid. What Davis did was to place an enormous tank of the stuff, some four hundred thousand litres, nearly a mile beneath the surface of the earth (which shields it against cosmic rays) in the Homestake gold mine located at Lead, South Dakota. Periodically, the tank is flushed to see if any of the chlorine has been converted into argon by the high-energy neutrinos. For many years, Davis was not able to detect *any* neutrinos—something that caused great consternation among astrophysicists. Recently, he has been finding some, but substantially fewer than the theory would call for. This has lead to a significant reexamination of the assumptions that presently comprise the theory of solar energy production. The resolution of this puzzle is still not clear, and the proposed explanations range from the idea that, for some reason, the sun is presently in a relatively quiescent state so far as the nuclear reactions are concerned, to the idea that the neutrino that arrives on earth is not the one that was originally produced, that it was transformed somehow from the so-called "electron" neutrino produced in the decay of the boron to one of the other types of neutrinos that are known to exist but which will not cause chlorine to transform into argon. Most physicists are convinced that however the puzzle is resolved it will lead to important new insights.

On September 14, 1939, Bethe and Rose Ewald, the daughter of his Stuttgart professor Paul Ewald, were married in New Rochelle, New York. "In 1935, when I got my visa to emigrate to America, I visited the Ewalds," Bethe told me. "And Rose, who was then seventeen, was present when I told Mrs. Ewald that I was going to America. Rose said, 'Why don't you take me along?' I didn't take her seriously, but two years later, when I was giving a lecture at Duke University, there she was. She had emigrated in 1936, and now she had a job as a housekeeper in Durham and was going to Duke part time. Rose had found out that I was coming to Duke, and at a banquet after the lecture she talked to me about trying to find a position for her father, who was also attempting to emigrate." He did manage to emigrate to England, in 1937, with his entire family. "Rose was then twenty, and I fell in love with her. I proposed to her in a letter as soon as I got home, but it took us two more years and a trip back to Europe on her part before we were married. In order to get a marriage license, we had to invent a domicile for her, since she had no fixed residence while going to college, and we picked New Rochelle, because it was the residence of the mathematician Richard Courant, an old family friend, who had helped Rose to immigrate and to find jobs before she went to college full time. We were married by a judge who recited the marriage ceremony in its briefest possible form—we thought it was a rehearsal. But he said now you are married, and so we are still. I handed him ten dollars, which he apparently considered more than his normal fee. After that, he was much friendlier. Richard Courant and his daughter Gertrude were there, along with Rose's housemother from Smith College, to which she had transferred in 1937, and the Tellers. Edward Teller, of course, was one of the two physicists at George Washington University who arranged the meeting that led to my work on the source of the energy of stars. In the years since we had both come to the United States, I had spent many happy hours at their home, in Washington, mostly in connection with scientific meetings. Edward and I had endless innumerable discussions on scientific problems. Later, Rose and I went for summer trips to the mountains with the Tellers. They were our best friends in this country." The friendship was one that would be severely tested in the years ahead.

PART II

Working
on the Bomb

Chapter 3

The A-Bomb

ONE of the most vivid accounts of the making of the American atomic bomb appears in *Manhattan Project*, a book by the journalist Stephane Groueff, which appeared in 1967. Toward the middle of it, there is a remarkable passage:

> Richard Feynman's voice could be heard from the far end of the corridor: "No, no, you're crazy!" His colleagues in the Los Alamos Theoretical Division looked up from their computers and exchanged knowing smiles. "There they go again!" one said. "The Battleship and the Mosquito Boat!"
> The "Battleship" was the division's leader, Hans Bethe, a tall, heavy-set German who was recognized as a sort of genius in theoretical physics. At the moment he was having one of his frequent discussions with Dick Feynman, the "Mosquito Boat," who, from the moment he started talking

physics, became completely oblivious of where he was and to whom he was talking. The imperturbable and meticulous Bethe solved problems by facing them squarely, analyzing them quietly and then plowing straight through them. He pushed obstacles aside like a battleship moving through the water.

Feynman, on the other hand, would interrupt him impatiently at nearly every sentence, either to shout his admiration or to express disagreement by irreverent remarks like "No, you're crazy!" or "That's nuts!" At each interruption Bethe would stop, then quietly and patiently explain why he was right. Feynman would calm down for a few minutes, only to jump in wildly again with "That's impossible, you're mad!" and again Bethe could calmly prove that it was not so.

These exchanges began in 1943, when Bethe was thirty-seven years old. Feynman, who had received his Ph.D. from Princeton the year before, was twenty-five. The average age of the technical personnel at Los Alamos was twenty-seven, and J. Robert Oppenheimer, the director of the entire project, was thirty-nine. "For me, Feynman sort of materialized from Princeton," Bethe told me. "I hadn't known about him, but Oppenheimer had. He was very lively from the beginning, but he didn't start insulting me until about two months after he came. The Mosquito Boat was delightful. I realized very quickly that he was something phenomenal. The first thing he did, since we had to integrate differential equations, and at that time had only hand computers, was to find an efficient method of integrating third-order differential equations numerically. It was very, very impressive. Then, within a month, we cooked up the formula for calculating the efficiency of a nuclear weapon. It is named the Bethe-Feynman formula, and it is still used. I thought Feynman perhaps the most ingenious man in the whole division, so we worked a great deal together. Very soon, I made him a group leader." In

1945, the younger man became an associate professor of theoretical physics at Cornell, where Bethe had been on the faculty since 1935. There Feynman did seminal work on the quantum mechanics of electrons and photons, for which he shared the Nobel Prize in Physics with Sin-itiro Tomonaga and Julian Schwinger in 1965. Feynman is now the Richard Chase Tolman Professor of Theoretical Physics at the California Institute of Technology.

Bethe had become an American citizen in March of 1941. Like many of the refugee scientists, he was concerned about what he saw as the inevitable American participation in a war against Germany. "After the fall of France, I was desperate to do something—to make some contribution to the war effort," he recalled. Not yet a citizen when France fell, Bethe was unable to get military clearance to work on classified projects, so he made up a project of his own. "I was still thinking in terms of the First World War—an old-fashioned war—so I chose the subject of the penetration of armor by projectiles," he said. "I went to the Encyclopædia Britannica and read the articles about armor penetration and armor manufacture. The theory of penetration given there seemed to be ad hoc—purely phenomenological. There was no logic to it at all. I have a friend, George Winter, who is a structural engineer. He recommended certain books to me, from which I learned elasticity theory and the theory of plastic deformation, and I became something of an expert in these matters. Partly with his help, I produced a theory of armor penetration—or, really, nonpenetration, because I was more interested in shielding than in penetration. I assumed that the Allied navies, for example, would be subect to German torpedoes, and I wanted to know what properties of the material used in the construction of ships the shielding depends on. It turned out that the shielding depends primarily on the yield stress of the material, and that the yield stress is much better in special steels, like tungsten, than it is in soft steel. My theory tied in with what the armor manufacturers had realized empirically, but it gave them the reason that their findings were correct, and it told them where to look next."

Having produced his theory, Bethe was at a loss as to what to do with it. In the winter of 1941, I. I. Rabi, who was in the Physics Department at Columbia, and whom Bethe had known since they were both students in Europe, sent him to the Army's Aberdeen Proving Ground, in Maryland, where he was shown some actual projectile damage in armor plate, but where no one was much interested in a general theory. However, the physicist Frederick Seitz, who was at that time a consultant at the Frankford Arsenal, in Philadelphia (he later became president of the National Academy of Science, and recently retired as president of Rockefeller University), had heard of Bethe's work, and after he had read the manuscript the arsenal had it published as a classified document. That meant that Bethe could no longer read it himself. Shortly after the war, Bethe encountered the paper again, and was pleased to see that it had gone through many reworkings, especially by the British and the Canadians, and also by people at other ballistics centers to which it had been sent; so the effort was not in vain. The episode is one illustration of the enormous range of problems in theoretical physics and engineering that Bethe has worked on successfully—a range that is beyond the reach of most contemporary physicists.

I asked him if he could somehow account for this facility.

"I have always been interested in solving problems in no matter what field, as long as I could apply mathematics to them," he replied. "For instance, when I was about fourteen I became interested in economics, and so I invented a way to calculate the effective yield of a bond to maturity.

There are tables for this, but I wanted to find—and did find—a nice, simple formula for doing it. My interest in many diverse problems and my ability to solve them are both a strength and a weakness in me. Many theoretical physicists choose one particular field and keep on trying to solve the problems related to that field, at whatever cost. Einstein is an example. After discovering general relativity, he wanted to unify the theories of gravitation and of electromagnetism. He failed in nearly forty years of trying, as many lesser physicists have failed who have set themselves one particular task. I admire the persistence of these people, especially since they usually want to solve the most profound problems. I have not tried to do this. I have usually picked problems that opportunity offered—problems that looked to me as if they required just my kind of ability and experience. I have at times worked consistently in one broad field, but while such work has given me great pleasure, it has usually been less successful."

The next wartime project that Bethe took on was in collaboration with Edward Teller, whom he had first met when they were students in Munich in the late nineteen-twenties. They had renewed their acquaintance when both went to England for a brief period after leaving Germany, and they became very close friends after they emigrated to the United States, in the nineteen-thirties. "We made several excursions from Washington where Teller lived," Bethe recalled, "into the Blue Ridge Mountains, to the seashore, and to other nice places. Wherever we went, we talked practically all the time—about physics, especially nuclear physics, and about politics. European politics—the Munich agreement, and the like. Still, it was not clear to me at the time how much Teller hated the Russians. That became clear only later—in the middle of the war." As a child in Budapest, Teller had witnessed the Communist revolution of Béla Kun and had heard about the atrocities committed, and soldiers had been billeted in the Tellers' apartment. These frightening childhood memories, it seems, have never left him. "Teller can be charming, and in those early days what I mostly knew was his charming side," Bethe told me. "I did know that he sometimes became moody when some problem was on his mind. He would shut up completely for an hour or so and think about it, no matter how many people or what people were around him. Well, I was quite happy to put up with it then. He also liked to go walking in the mountains. We took an extensive trip through the Western mountains in 1937. Teller always used to say, 'This is almost as beautiful as the High Tatra'— mountains that he climbed in his youth."

In the summer of 1940, Bethe was teaching at Stanford University and Teller was on vacation in the California mountains, and the two of them got together and decided to visit Theodor von Kármán, a celebrated Hungarian-born aeronautical engineer and physicist, who was a close friend of Teller's and who was then on the faculty of the California Institute of Technology. The idea was to ask him to give them some war-related research to do. Von Kármán suggested that they study certain aspects of the theory of shock waves. A shock wave is produced when, for example, a projectile moves through a gas, such as air, at a speed greater than the speed of sound in that gas. When this happens, a thin wave is established in front of the projectile, and as this wave travels into the gas it causes abrupt changes in the gas, such as changes in its temperature and pressure: it "shocks" the gas. Bethe and Teller studied the problem of how the equilibrium of the gas is reestablished behind the shock wave. "We produced a formal theory of that, and it was published by the Aberdeen Proving Ground,"

Bethe said. "It was much more useful than my paper on armor penetration, because later it became the basis for the use of shock waves to investigate the properties of gases. One of the people who did a lot of work on this was Arthur Kantrowitz, a student of Teller's, who became the founder and director of the Avco Everett Research Laboratory, in Everett, Massachusetts, near Boston. He became interested in shock waves in 1941 and, with Teller's guidance, did his thesis on the subject. Later, his interest in shock waves led him to play an important part in solving the problem of the reentry of missiles into the atmosphere. In a way, all this took off from my joint paper with Teller, which showed how the gas behind a shock wave would gradually come into equilibrium."

That summer, at a meeting of the American Physical Society in Seattle, Bethe had his first prolonged encounter with Oppenheimer, who was then professor of theoretical physics both at the California Institute of Technology and at the University of California at Berkeley. They had met before, at a scientific conference in Germany in 1929, but the meeting had not been a felicitous one. Bethe had presented a paper, and Oppenheimer had made a cutting remark about it, which later turned out to be simply incorrect. Then, one evening in Seattle, Oppenheimer gave what Bethe remembers as a "beautifully eloquent speech" about the disaster that had overtaken the world—the fall of France—and how essential it was now to rescue Western civilization. His speech was a great surprise to many people who had known him for some time. "He had had sympathies to the far left—mostly, I believe, on humanitarian grounds," Bethe explained. "The Hitler-Stalin pact had confused most people with Communist sympathies into staying completely aloof from the war against Germany until the Nazis invaded Russia, in 1941. But Oppenheimer was so deeply impressed by the fall of France that this displaced everything else in his mind."

By 1940, a few physicists in the United States had begun to build an atomic bomb—or, at least, to see if one could be built—but with minimal support from the government. In January of 1939, the Danish physicist Niels Bohr had arrived in the United States with the news that nuclear fission had been discovered the month before by Otto Hahn and Fritz Strassmann in Germany. There were theoretical physicists who might well have predicted fission some years before its discovery. Indeed, as early as 1934 the physicist Enrico Fermi and his group in Rome were doing experiments that would have certainly revealed fission if anyone had thought to look for it. In one experiment, they were bombarding a thorium target with neutrons in order to study its interactions with the neutrons. They expected to produce nuclei comparable in mass to those of thorium. They had put a metal foil in front of the target. Unknown to them, the neutrons produced fission of the thorium, but the foil stopped the fission products from reaching their detector. Emilio Segrè, a Nobel Prize-winning nuclear physicist, who is now professor emeritus at Berkeley, was with Fermi then. He remarked recently, "The foil never fell down." If it had, fission might have been discovered in 1934. The person most likely to have predicted fission was Bohr himself. In 1936, he had invented a successful model of the atomic nucleus which was known as the liquid-drop model. In its simplest version, the nucleus is pictured as a spherical droplet composed of neutrons and protons. The nuclear force that acts among these particles tends to keep the droplet together, while the electric force that acts among the protons tends to push the droplet apart. In elements such as fermium and californium, which are even heavier than uranium and plutonium, there is a strong tendency for this droplet to break up spontaneously—to fission— into two relatively light nuclei. In such elements as uranium and plutonium, this "spontaneous" fission occurs, but only as a very slow process. However, it can be made to occur rapidly if the nucleus is bombarded by a projectile, such as a neutron. That is, the tendency for these nuclei to assume an elongated shape and split apart is enhanced by "shaking" them—irradiating them with neutrons. (Fission can also be caused by the irradiation of other particles, such as gamma-rays-energetic light quanta.) Fissionable materials respond differently to neutrons of different energies. U-238, the abundant isotope of uranium, fissions only when it is irradiated by "fast" neutrons—those having an energy of a million electron volts or so—while the rare isotope U-235 responds to "slow," or "thermal," neutrons, which have energies of a few hundredths of an electron volt. This fact, which is crucial in the design of nuclear reactors, has to do with the intricacies of the nuclear force that holds a nucleus together.

Bohr made extensive use of the liquid-drop model to explain nuclear reactions. This work was well understood by Bethe, who at about the same time was writing three monumental review articles on physics—the first on atomic physics, the second on solid-state physics, and the last on nuclear physics. It was also known to Fermi, who was actually doing experiments on neutron reactions, and to other nuclear physicists as well. But no one had posed the right question—whether the model would allow nuclear fission. "None of us stopped to think," Bethe told me. "If we had, we could have very easily calculated the stability of nuclei against deformations, and we would have predicted fission. But none of us did that simple exercise. It was terribly stupid." Hahn himself, after he had done his experiments, was all but unable to believe his results. He had expected that when one of his neutrons irradiated uranium there would be a nuclear reaction but that the final product would be something like radium, which also has a heavy nucleus. Instead, he kept seeing barium, which has a nucleus of about half the mass of a uranium nucleus. The technique that Hahn was using involved adding barium salt to the reaction product. Barium and radium have similar chemical properties and precipitate out of a sulphate solution together. This enabled him to analyze chemically a minute amount of the reaction product. But the more analysis he did, the more it began to appear that the reaction product *was* barium. Fission is a complicated process. There are at least thirty different ways in which a U-235 nucleus, for example, can split when it absorbs a slow neutron. Each of these splittings produces two lighter nuclei and some number of neutrons. The process that Hahn observed had as one of its products a radioactive isotope of xenon. It rapidly decayed into an isotope of cesium, which, in turn, decayed into the barium isotope that Hahn identified. In December of 1938, Hahn wrote to a former collaborator, Lise Meitner, who had just gone to Sweden to escape the Nazis, "Our 'radium' isotope is behaving just like barium." She replied, "Your radium results are really very disconcerting: a process using slow neutrons that yields barium?! . . . At present it seems to me very difficult to accept that there is such a drastic breaking-up [of the uranium nucleus], but we have experienced so many surprises in nuclear physics that one cannot dismiss this by saying simply: 'It's not possible!' " Indeed, soon afterward she and a nephew of hers, the physicist Otto Frisch, who coined the term "fission," used Bohr's liquid-drop model to show that such a process could take place, and that a great deal of energy would be released when it did.

All this occurred just before the war. One can only wonder what would have happened if fission had been discovered a few years earlier or a few years later—and, considering how the discovery did get made, this might well have happened. Every aspect of our present attitude toward nuclear fission can be traced to the fact that it was discovered just as the war began and that this country, as things turned out, was the one that was in a position sufficiently isolated from the fighting to develop its applications. From almost the instant that Hahn made his discovery, German nuclear physicists began actively studying how to make a fission bomb—and so did Japanese nuclear physicists, though less intensively. What would it have meant if this work had secretly got started in Germany or Japan a few years earlier?

The work in this country started at a leisurely pace, and in the beginning it was carried out, on the whole, as simply another branch of academic physics. In 1939, the physicists Leo Szilard and Walter Zinn, working at Columbia, showed in an experiment that in the uranium fission stimulated by a neutron, several neutrons would be released along with the heavy fission fragments. This meant that in principle a chain reaction was possible—that is, a reaction in which the fission process would be self-sustaining. And in 1939, Bohr and the theoretical physicist J. A. Wheeler, who were both at Princeton, wrote a fundamental paper on nuclear fission using the liquid-drop model, in which they showed that slow neutrons did not cause the most common isotope of uranium—U-238—to fission but did cause the rare light isotope U-235 to fission. Since U-235 occurs only in small amounts in natural uranium, this result made it clear that using uranium fission as an energy source was going to involve high technology—the technology of isotope separation. (Or else it would involve the manufacture of plutonium, an element that does not under normal circumstances exist naturally. Or it would involve the manufacture of large amounts of heavy hydrogen which, as we shall see, enables one to use natural uranium in plutonium-manufacturing reactors.) This, together with the fact that no one knew whether a successful controlled chain reaction could be made to occur in practice (during the war, the German nuclear physicists were never able to build a reactor that would make such a reaction work), convinced many physicists, among them Rabi and Bethe, that working on a nuclear weapon was essentially futile as a way to influence the outcome of the war.

"In 1939, Szilard tried to ban all publication of work having to do with fission," Bethe told me. "He felt that one could use fission to make a bomb. I considered the possibility of an atomic bomb so remote that I completely refused to have anything to do with it until three years later. I knew that some of my friends, like Fermi and Teller and Eugene Wigner, were working on it, but I heard only the vaguest rumors about it. Separating isotopes of such a heavy element was clearly a very difficult thing to do, and I thought we would never succeed in any practical way." Two isotopes differ from each other only in the number of neutrons in the nucleus; the number of protons is the same. The number of protons indirectly determines the chemistry of the atom, since it determines the number of electrons that orbit the nucleus, and it is the forces among the electrons in different atoms which makes possible the chemical binding between them. Two isotopes have essentially the same chemistry, and so they generally cannot be separated chemically. Methods must be used that take advantage of the different weights of the two nuclei. In a heavy nucleus, this difference in weight is only a very small fraction of the weight of the nucleus itself. That is why the separation process is so difficult for, say, the isotopes of uranium. "I was also very doubtful whether people would be able to develop a chain-reacting pile—a reactor," Bethe said. "This opinion was changed only in 1942, when I was invited to join the Manhattan Project and was shown, mainly by Teller, what had actually been done. Teller and Fermi had moved to Chicago, and I went there, to the Met Lab, and saw that Fermi was well on the way to making a chain-reacting pile. He had a setup under one of the stands in Stagg Field—in a squash court—with tremendous stacks of graphite, and had got to the stage where he could actually calculate the rate of neutron multiplication in a uranium pile that had a graphite moderator." The graphite acts as a moderator by slowing the neutrons down after they have been released in the fission. Both ordinary water and heavy water, as well as other materials are also used for that purpose. With these moderators a reactor, like Fermi's, was able to use natural uranium; the only kind then available. "I then became convinced that the atomic-bomb project was real, and that it would probably work."

On December 7, 1941, Bethe received his clearance to work on classified military projects, but the first project he was asked to work on had nothing to do with the bomb. It was radar, which was being developed at the Radiation Laboratory of the Massachusetts Institute of Technology. In the beginning, the laboratory farmed out some of its theoretical-physics projects, and Bethe organized a small group of young co-workers at Cornell to help him with the project that he had been asked to undertake. The group included Schwinger and Robert Marshak. Bethe had known Schwinger since 1925, when he was discovered, at the age of sixteen, by Rabi at Columbia. Bethe and Schwinger had kept in touch, and Schwinger, who had meanwhile taken a job at Purdue University, came to Cornell several times to consult Bethe, and then moved to M.I.T. in 1943. Schwinger stayed there throughout the war and became the guiding genius in the theoretical development of radar. Bethe at that time invented what is now known as the Bethe coupler —a device used to measure the propagation of electromagnetic waves in waveguides. Bethe remained in Cambridge until March of 1943, and while he was there he received a phone call from Oppenheimer asking him to work on the atomic bomb.

Los Alamos did not begin to function as a laboratory until April of 1943, but well before then Oppenheimer had essentially taken charge of the work that would have to be done before nuclear material could be assembled into a bomb. In the spring of 1942, he had been appointed by the federal Office of Scientific Research and Development to lead the theoretical side of the effort to assemble the bomb. He organized a summer study group at Berkeley of those physicists he thought would be most useful in this work— Bethe among them. "Somehow, Oppenheimer managed to convey discreetly over the telephone what he had in mind," Bethe told me. "My curiosity got the best of me, and so I agreed to go."

On the way, Bethe stopped in Chicago to pick up Teller, which is when he saw Fermi's work on the graphite reactor. "We had a compartment on the train to California, so we could talk freely," Bethe went on. "Teller told me about the idea of making plutonium in the reactor and using the plutonium in a nuclear weapon." In a reactor fuelled by uranium, plutonium is manufactured automatically. When U-235 fissions, the neutrons that are emitted along with the heavy fission fragments cause both further fissions and ordinary nuclear reactions. Most of the uranium in the reactor is in the form of U-238, and when one of the released neutrons collides with a U-238 nucleus it can initiate a sequence of processes that results in the transmutation of the U-238 into a readily fissionable isotope of plutonium—Pu-239. (Thus, in these reactors the fuel supply regenerates itself to a degree—an important consideration in estimating the economy of using reactors to produce power.) The great advantage of using plutonium rather than U-235 in manufacturing weapons is that plutonium can be chemically separated from uranium, since it is a different atom with entirely different chemical properties.

"Teller told me that the fission bomb was all well and good and, essentially, was now a sure thing," Bethe said. "In reality, the work had hardly begun. Teller likes to jump to conclusions. He said that what we really should think about was the possibility of igniting deuterium by a fission weapon—the hydrogen bomb. Well, the whole thing was far more difficult than we thought then. About three-quarters of our time that summer was occupied with thinking about the possibility of a hydrogen super-weapon. We encountered one difficulty after another, and came up with one solution after another—but the difficulties were clearly in the majority. My wife knew vaguely what we were talking about, and on a walk in the mountains in Yosemite National Park she asked me to consider carefully whether I really wanted to continue to work on this. Finally, I decided to do it. It was clear that the super bomb, especially, was a terrible thing. But the fission bomb had to be done, because the Germans were presumably doing it."

To what extent the Germans were actually working towards the manufacture of a bomb is not clear, but they were certainly working feverishly on the exploitation of uranium fission. (The Japanese, too, by then had the beginnings of an atomic-bomb project.) Indeed, the most distinguished German physicist, Werner Heisenberg, whom Bethe had known for nearly twenty years, told him in 1948, on the occasion of Bethe's first visit to Germany after the war, that he had been working on uranium fission full time (he had been the director of the most important laboratory in the German project), and he gave Bethe three reasons why he had done so. "He said that his main aim had been to save the lives of German physicists," Bethe remarked. "He wanted to do something that would appear to contribute to the war effort and would keep his physicist friends in Germany and away from the Russian front. Clearly, even if they had been able to make only a reactor, that in itself would have been a major achievement for Germany. The second reason he gave was that he believed making an atomic bomb was far beyond the means of any country during the war. I think that at the time that was his honest opinion. He said he simply could not believe that any country, even the United States, had the money and the industrial capacity to see such a project through to the end during the war. And for Germany, of course, the project was much more difficult than for us, because its resources were smaller than ours to begin with and were also strained by constant air raids. His third reason was that in 1942 he had come to the conclusion that the Germans should win the war. That struck me as a very naïve statement. He said he knew that the Germans had committed terrible atrocities against the populations on the Eastern Front—in Poland and Russia—and to some extent in the West as well. He concluded that the Allies would never forgive this and would destroy Germany as a nation—that they would treat Germany about the way the Romans had treated Carthage. This, he said to himself, should not happen; therefore, Germany should win the war, and then the good Germans would take care of the Nazis. It is unbelievable that a man who has made some of the greatest contributions to modern physics should have been that naïve. But he seems to have said similar things to people during the war. He never mentioned anything to me about the morality of making a nuclear weapon. In 1939, though, Heisenberg was certainly anti-Nazi. He had been attacked by the Nazi press for being too friendly to Jews and for teaching 'Jewish physics'—including Einstein's theory of relativity."

The Germans' failure to make an atomic bomb was in a sense remarkable, for German physicists did have a complete understanding of what an atomic bomb was and how to go about making one; that is, they understood the two basic methods of producing bombs—using uranium enriched with isotope U-235 and using plutonium manufactured in a reactor. In fact, both methods were described at a conference that the German nuclear physicists held with representatives of the government and the military in February of 1942—several months before the Manhattan Project was created. However, the German scientists were never able to bridge the gap between theory and the completion of even the first step—the building of a working reactor. There were several reasons for this. In the first place, the organization of German science was hierarchical. An exchange of the type that Bethe had with Feynman—between a senior scientist and a new Ph.D., and on an almost daily basis—would have been inconceivable among the authority-minded German scientists. Thus, in January of 1941, when Walther Bothe, the leading German experimental nuclear physicist, made a mistake in an experiment, no one thought of challenging it, or even thought it worthwhile to repeat the experiment. His result was accepted without question.

Bothe was trying to measure the properties of graphite as a neutron absorber. He was doing experiments of the sort that Fermi did on graphite a little later. But Bothe did not realize that his graphite was not sufficiently purified; industrial graphite often contains substantial boron impurities, and boron is an especially strong neutron absorber. Bothe drew the conclusion that pure graphite absorbed more neutrons than it actually does, and so ruled out the use of graphite as a moderator for a nuclear reactor. This mistake proved to be fatal to the German's attempt to make a reactor. The reason is that once they had ruled out graphite—an easily obtainable substance—they turned to heavy water as a moderator. Heavy water composes about a hundredth of a percent of the content of ordinary water, and it is separated from ordinary water by electrolysis—an electrical process in which the water is decomposed into its components, hydrogen or heavy hydrogen and oxygen. (Ordinary water will not do as well as a moderator, because the sole proton in ordinary hydrogen tends to capture the neutrons instead of simply slowing them down by collisions. In heavy hydrogen, this proton already has a neutron partner, and so is much less effective in capturing neutrons. The oxygen is not an effective capturer in either case.) As it happened, the only place in Western Europe capable of manufacturing heavy water on the scale needed was a hydroelectric plant at Vemork, in southern Norway. Once the Allies understood the significance of this plant, it was attacked both from the air and by commandos, and the Germans were never able to acquire the amount of heavy water needed for a reactor.

Another of the German's difficulties arose from the fact that Heisenberg was not really an engineer. "Although Heisenberg was a superb theoretical physicist, he didn't have the practical sense that, say, Fermi had," Bethe told me. "So his calculation of the volume of heavy water that he needed was wrong. He thought he had acquired half the volume needed when he had only a fifth. Fermi, on the other hand, could calculate to within a few percent. Thus, insufficient competence played a considerable part in the failure of the Germans' project. In addition, different groups were working on it separately. Instead of having one centrally directed group split up among different laboratories, as we had, they had five unrelated groups working against one another, because each group wanted to have the use of whatever uranium was available. At Berkeley in the summer of 1942, our little group discussed the Germans. We knew that Heisenberg was interested in making a bomb and that there were physicists in Germany working on it, and so, as we saw it, there was just no question that the Germans would do it. We felt that we had to continue our work, and we produced quite a lot of results that summer, some on fission weapons and some on the super."

Part of the Berkeley group's information about the Germans' intentions came from Bohr. In October of 1941, Heisenberg, on his own initiative, made a visit to Copenhagen to see Bohr. The reason for this visit is not clear. It occurred just after Heisenberg had become certain that—in principle, at least—a bomb could be made. Perhaps he wanted to reach some understanding with Bohr that neither side would make a bomb, or perhaps he had some more devious intent. In any case, he succeeded only in convincing Bohr that the Germans were on the verge of making a bomb. He gave Bohr a drawing, of which Bethe said, "Later on, at Los Alamos, this drawing was transmitted to us by Bohr. It was clearly a drawing of a reactor, but when we saw it our conclusion was that these Germans were totally crazy—did they want to throw a reactor down on London?" In retrospect, the German scientists were not crazy at all. They knew perfectly well what to do with a reactor, and this drawing was of the reactor that Heisenberg tried throughout the war to build but was unable to finish. Apparently, he hoped that by giving Bohr the drawing he would lead Bohr to conclude that the Germans were not building a bomb.

During the summer of 1942, Bethe came to know Oppenheimer well. "It was perhaps the closest I ever got to him," he remarked to me, "because once we got to Los Alamos he had so much to do that we saw much less of each other than we had during that summer. I was very much impressed by him, and my feelings were entirely positive. There was no question that he was our leader. Perhaps he didn't contribute as much original thought as Teller and I did, but he had a far better critical faculty than any of the rest of us. His grasp of problems was immediate —he could often understand an entire problem after he had heard a single sentence. Incidentally, one of the difficulties that he had in dealing with people was that he expected them to have the same faculty. I think he really was a great man. After that summer, I went back to the Radiation Laboratory at M.I.T. We had come to the conclusion that designing the actual bomb would require a new, separate laboratory, and for a while Oppenheimer was in negotiation with General Leslie R. Groves, who had been appointed to head the entire enterprise, about where it should be located and how it should be organized. In November, Los Alamos was decided on, and Oppie asked all of us to join him there. Very soon, we did. There was some flap about whether we would have to join the Army in order to do so—an idea that few of us liked very much. Rabi and R. F. Bacher—formerly a colleague of Bethe's at Cornell and later Provost of Cal. Tech.—"gave Oppie some fatherly advice to the effect that the lab would never work if there were to be a military chain of command; it would make the exchange of ideas much too formal, and hence too slow. He had agreed in the beginning to have all of us go into uniform, but under this pressure he reconsidered, and told General Groves that none of his best people would come unless they could remain civilians. And so Groves agreed—grudgingly, but he agreed. There was actually a written agreement between Groves and James Conant, the civilian head of the Manhattan project, that Los Alamos should be a civilian laboratory until the bomb was actually manu-factured and delivered—when it would become military—but this part of the agreement was never implemented. There was another flap because E. O. Lawrence, who was director of the uranium project there at Berkeley, wanted one of his people, Edwin McMillan, to be the director. But Groves very wisely decided that the director had to be Oppenheimer. Nobody else would have made as good a director."

Bethe arrived at Los Alamos in April of 1943. His wife, Rose, who had been made the Manhattan Project's housing officer, had already been there for ten days. "I went by train to a place called Lamy, New Mexico, which was the railroad station for Santa Fe," Bethe told me. "Later on, there was a story about some people who went to the rail-road station in Princeton to buy tickets to Lamy, and the ticket seller told them, 'Don't go there. Twenty people have already gone there, and not one of them has ever come back.' Lamy was a wilderness—a few houses and a bar, and nothing else. The whole business struck me as very un-likely. My wife met me in a government car, and we drove through the early-spring desert. There were some bloom-ing fruit trees, but mostly it was stark desert. Nowadays, I find the drive very beautiful, but at that time those dry mountains and the desert seemed rather frightening. I kept imagining myself walking through the desert without a drop of water. After leaving the desert, we took a muddy road that wound its way up the mountainside. At any moment, the car could have fallen into the gorge. This didn't scare me much, but it made it seem more and more unlikely that we were driving to a big laboratory. Up on the top, it was very beautiful, with the pinewoods behind Los Alamos and the snow-covered mountains on the other side of the Rio Grande Valley. In addition, there was the bluest sky imaginable, and the clearest air. Then, in the middle of all this, they had built shacks. I can describe them only as shacks. But these were the laboratory facilities. Later, they built apartment houses, which were supposed to last only for 'the duration' but actually lasted twenty-five years, and would still be serviceable if they hadn't been torn down. When I first arrived, we lived in the old Lodge." Los Alamos had been the site of the Los Alamos Ranch School for Boys, and the Lodge had been one of the school's principal structures. There were about a hundred people on the site then, and many of them lived outside Los Alamos in various lodgings and had to commute twenty miles or more to work. Oppenheimer had originally thought that thirty people would be enough to design the bomb. Rabi and Bacher persuaded him that he would need at least five hundred, and by the end of the war there were five thousand technical people working at the site.

Once it was clear that the number of people was going to grow, Oppenheimer became convinced—and Rabi and Bacher helped convince him—that the laboratory would have to be organized into divisions and that within each division there should be several groups. Bacher was asked to head the Experimental Physics Division; a twenty-six-year-old chemist named Joseph Kennedy, who had participated in the discovery of plutonium, was named head of the Chemical Division; Captain William Parsons, a Regular Navy officer, became head of the Ordnance Division; and Bethe was named head of the Theoretical Division. From the moment Bethe was given this appointment, both his and Oppenheimer's relations with Teller deteriorated. "That I was named to head the division was a severe blow to Teller, who had worked on the bomb project almost from the day of its inception and considered himself, quite rightly, as having seniority over everyone then at Los Alamos, including Oppenheimer," Bethe told me. "Why, then, was he not made division leader? One might say that scientifically Teller is overfertile. New ideas and new combinations of old ideas simply tumble out of his brain. It is this gift that enabled him to discover, in 1951, a new approach to making the hydrogen bomb. In 1943, Oppenheimer and his advisers felt that my more plodding but steadier approach to life and science would serve the project better at that stage of its development, where decisions had to be adhered to and detailed calculations had to be carried through, and where, therefore, a good deal of administrative work was inevitable. Also, it was the consensus of the senior people at the laboratory that we would not go into the super bomb—except, perhaps, theoretically. Everyone was to concentrate on making a workable fission weapon. Teller didn't like that, either, because he had come to Los Alamos with the idea of continuing his work on the super and of having a lot of experimental people to work with him."

Teller himself has commented to Stanley A. Blumberg and Gwinn Owens, the authors of his biography *Energy and Conflict*, "When Los Alamos was established as a separate entity from the Met Lab, one of the arguments was that we would work on the fusion bomb as well as on the fission bomb. We actually didn't, and this was certainly something that I was unhappy about. Furthermore, Bethe was given the job to organize the effort, and in my opinion —in which I well may have been wrong—he overorganized it. It was much too much of a military organization, a line organization."

For many of the young couples who were arriving at Los Alamos, this was the first time they had had the prospect of a steady income and of living in one place for a reasonable length of time, with assured housing—even if their choice of housing was severely limited. General Groves had decreed that a family needed a living room, a kitchen, and a bath, and one bedroom for parents, one for boys, and one for girls—if there were no children to begin with, a second bedroom for the first child. Perhaps partly for that reason, one notable aspect of life at Los Alamos was that many of the couples had babies. "It was the 'in' thing to do," Bethe said, half seriously. "It seemed to be a very fertile atmosphere." The Bethes' son, Henry, was born in 1944. Today, Henry, a banker in New York City, is married and has a son himself—the Bethe's first grandchild. The Bethe's daughter, Monica, was born in 1945. She lives in Kyoto and has become an expert on Japanese Noh theatre.

A great deal has been written about the scientific and engineering work that was done at Los Alamos; in fact, there appears to be a widespread belief that so much has been published in the open literature that almost anyone with a pocket calculator and some plutonium can make a bomb. This notion was reinforced recently when it was reported that two students, one at M.I.T. and the other at Princeton, had actually designed a workable bomb simply by going to the library and digging out the unclassified reports. (It was also reported that Pakistan was interested in recruiting the services of the Princeton student.) With this in mind, I put a question to Bethe: Suppose one had available all the open literature on making a bomb, including these student papers, *and* one had all the enriched uranium or plutonium that one needed—where would one be in the construction of an atomic bomb?

His answer was "Nowhere." Though the general principles involved in making such a device are well known and are available in the open literature, he explained, the details, which are extremely intricate, are not. "I have seen the paper of the Princeton student, and to the professional it is not impressive," Bethe said. "He presents with great seriousness a calculation of the energy yield of a bomb, assuming a certain amount of fissile material, and assuming the efficiency of the nuclear reaction—a grade-school exercise in multiplication—but he never gives any argument for assuming this particular efficiency, which in fact is much too high for an amateur bomb. He mentions a few types of explosives that could be used to assemble the fissile material, but he does not discuss the intricate shapes in which the explosive has to be cast. To cast the correct shapes, and to prove experimentally that they were indeed correct, took us months at Los Alamos, with hundreds of technicians, and this was just one of the many problems that are not discussed in the open literature."

I asked Bethe what such a student—or a terrorist—would need to go the rest of the way.

His answer was rather involved. "The critical mass of plutonium is available in the open literature," he said. The critical mass is that mass at which a fission chain reaction will just maintain itself. With larger masses, the rate of fissions will increase rapidly. This means that if a fissionable material like plutonium is assembled in masses larger than the critical mass, the rate of fissions will be so great that the energy production will run away—explode. A plutonium bomb can be made, in principle, with about ten kilograms of plutonium. In an ordinary power reactor, the fuel elements are not plutonium but uranium—a mixture of U-235 and U-238. It is the U-235 that undergoes the fissions, and the U-235 is mixed with the non-fissionable U-238 in a proportion of about three percent U-235 to ninety-seven percent U-238. In this mixture a power reactor can never explode like a bomb, no matter what one does to it.

Bethe continued, "One can also find out how the plutonium is to be surrounded. The easiest way to build a bomb is to have the plutonium at the center, surrounded by uranium, with a high explosive surrounding the uranium. All this information is readily available. But then one needs to machine the plutonium; this is difficult and dangerous. In a reactor, plutonium is usually in the form of a mixture of uranium oxide and plutonium oxide. Thus, the first job would be to separate the two oxides; for this work, one would need a very skilled inorganic chemist, such as one would find at a first-rate university. Next, the student or terrorist would have to decide whether to reduce the plutonium oxide to the pure metal—another job for a skilled chemist—or to use the oxide in the bomb. In the latter case, the required critical mass is always larger, and the energy yield of the bomb smaller. The metal, on the other hand, is pyrophoric, as is uranium metal, unless it is very carefully made into a completely dense, uniform ingot—a job for a metallurgist. A pyrohoric metal is one that catches fire spontaneously. Either the metal or the oxide would have to be machined into a spherical shape. The machining of either metal or oxide is also dangerous, because if even a small amount of plutonium dust is breathed in, it can cause cancer. The surrounding uranium would also have to be machined. And then comes the explosive."

The explosive is wrapped around the metal core and is detonated at several places simultaneously to cause the core to compress and reach the critical mass rapidly. Inside the core is an "initiator"—a neutron source—whose protective covering is removed by this explosion. The intiator provides the neutrons that get the chain reaction started. "During the war, as I've mentioned, it took us many months to do this, and we had the great explosives expert George Kistiakowsky as the leader, working with hundreds of technicians," Bethe said. "The first experiments on the implosion had absolutely awful results. Instead of giving a uniform speed to the metal being propelled by the explosive, they produced all sorts of jets and irregularities. It turned out that the best way to get rid of the jets was to make explosive lenses, but that only shifted the problem to another place—to the casting and machining of an explosive lens. It took them a long time to get uniform casting without bubbles. If you have a bubble, the explosive will not produce a uniform detonation wave but will again give jets and push the metal inside into some irregular shape. It took months and months before our Explosives Division learned to cast big chunks of explosives in a uniform manner and make the process reliable. Plastic explosives, they tell me, are what a terrorist might try to use. Perhaps so. But I doubt very much whether a plastic explosive is sufficiently uniform in density and detonation velocity to satisfy the criteria for making a convergent detonation. Another difficult problem with the explosive is to achieve simultaneity of explosion for all the detonators. There may be ten or more detonators, and they must be synchronized to a fraction of a millionth of a second. This is far from easy to test. By the way, I read a booklet published by the Indians describing their project—published, mind you, a year or two before they exploded their bomb. It sounded just like Los Alamos. They did much the same experiments, and they obviously did them well. They had the same kind of measuring apparatus—perhaps a little better—and, as at Los Alamos, thousands of people were engaged in the experimentation. The same was true of the Chinese, the Russians, the French, and the British."

I told Bethe that it sounded to me as if the minimum number of people that could possibly make a bomb, given the material, was something like an M.I.T. gone mad.

"Not quite," he said. "Although it would have to be a major effort, directed by first-class people from six or more different departments. One department would not be enough, and if the number of scientists were small and there were no technicians it would take them a long time, during which they would have to keep it secret. It might not be necessary to do everything as carefully as it was done at Los Alamos, but there would be a large number of complicated things to do, all of which must be done right. It requires breadth of knowledge to understand just what these are and how to do them, and great care in doing them. Failing to do these things could result in a dud or in an accident fatal to some of the people concerned. For these reasons, I think it totally unlikely that a terrorist group could make a bomb. It is not impossible, but they would have to recruit a substantial number of people who are at once fanatical and very competent. There are so many easier and quicker forms of terrorism. But when it comes to nations, I believe that a bomb is now within the capacity of half the nations in the world, including Pakistan, Iran, Argentina, Brazil, and, probably, Venezuela, Chile, and Egypt. There are still many smaller and less developed countries for which it would be almost impossible unless they imported a large number of foreign scientists."

I once heard Oppenheimer discuss Los Alamos, and he remarked that in the beginning he was worried that the general development of the bomb would be so simple that the group at Los Alamos would get finished way ahead of the groups that were manufacturing the U-235, at Oak Ridge, or the plutonium, at the Hanford reactor, in the state of Washington. When the first sample of plutonium reached Los Alamos, on February 2, 1945, however, the laboratory was just barely ready to use it. On July 16th, Fat Man, the first plutonium bomb, was exploded in the test at Alamogordo, and four weeks later the war was over.

With the explosion at Alamogordo, the physicists were confronted with the stark reality of atomic weaponry—not that they had been uaware, while they were building the bomb, of what they were doing, and of its consequences for the future. Indeed, Oppenheimer had spent part of his time throughout the Los Alamos period in consultation with Niels Bohr, who, because of his worldwide scientific reputation, was there under a pseudonym—Nicholas Baker —attempting to plan a postwar approach to nuclear weapons and nuclear power. But the energies of the working physicists were by and large consumed by the demands of the work on the bomb itself.

"I had been absorbed in the work, but as soon as the test was successful at Alamogordo I joined the discussions that were then being held by many people at the laboratory about what to do with the bomb and with atomic energy in general, and especially about whether it should be under civilian or military control in the United States," Bethe said. "At that time, the idea of international control was a common subject of discussion, and I think everybody at the laboratory was in favor of it. Oppenheimer, when he left the laboratory, gave a moving farewell lecture, in which he spoke of the problems of the future.* I became much involved in the formation of the Federation of American Scientists, which grew out of the discussions of our group at Los Alamos and the groups that had worked on the bomb elsewhere. Eventually, the ideas that resulted from these discussions—especially those of Niels Bohr—were incorporated in the Acheson-Lilienthal Report, which was written largely by Oppenheimer, and was issued in March of 1946. That report stated the reasons for having international control of atomic energy. It was presented to the United Nations, but the Russians, who were already far advanced in their own atomic-bomb work, turned it down."

During the late forties, Bethe was deeply involved in the movement among atomic scientists both for the civilian control of atomic energy in this country and for some form of international control. He testified before the Senate committee that was framing the law to establish the Atomic Energy Commission. He gave talks favoring international control, and he joined with other scientists in contributing to a widely circulated pamphlet entitled "One World or None," which warned of the possibility of nuclear war. In an article in this pamphlet, which he wrote with Frederick Seitz, he and Seitz pointed out that the "secret" of the atomic bomb could not be kept, and that a determined nation could produce a bomb in five years. (Although the Soviet Union was not explicitly mentioned, this was the nation that they had in mind.) Their article contradicted testimony given by General Groves and Vannevar Bush, who had been director of the wartime Office

---

* This lecture has now been published along with many of Oppenheimer's letters in *Robert Oppenheimer: Letters and Recollections*, edited by Alice Kimball Smith and Charls Weiner.

of Scientific Research and Development, that the secret could be kept for a long time. The Soviet Union exploded its first nuclear device in 1949—just about when Bethe and Seitz had said it would. Bethe and the other scientists who had been at Los Alamos worked intensely to try to educate the general public concerning the implications of nuclear weapons. One of the fears of the atomic scientists was that governments might consider the bomb just another weapon and, ignorant of its tremendous destructive effects, might start a war. "Since I expected Russia to have the atomic bomb within five years, I feared that we might have a nuclear holocaust that would destroy the civilizations of both countries," Bethe told me. "Fortunately, by now governments have learned to respect nuclear weapons and have scrupulously avoided their use. Our 1946 warning has become part of common knowledge."

Bethe remained at Los Alamos only until January of 1946. He was concerned over the fact that a generation of physicists had been lost, because their education had been disrupted by the war. "I wanted to get back to Cornell and do physics again," he said. "I thought that it was important to teach—that we needed new physicists and that my primary purpose in life was to be in a university." This notion brought him into disagreement with Teller once more. At that time, Teller was certain that the Russians were as great a danger as the Germans had been, and he wanted the Los Alamos laboratory to remain intact and work on the super. Teller particularly wanted Bethe to remain, and, indeed, to succeed Oppenheimer as the director of the laboratory, but Bethe refused. It was with a sense of relief that he returned to Cornell. Ithaca had, among other amenities, fresh water that actually came out of faucets. "In that last winter at Los Alamos, we had a terrible water shortage," Bethe told me. "The water supply had been built for the Los

Alamos school, which had maybe fifty people, and there were several thousand of us. There just wasn't any water. We got water delivered in trucks that had previously been used to transport gasoline, so the water generally tasted of gasoline. It may not have been bad for our health, but it certainly wasn't pleasant."

Over the next few years, Bethe served on various government committees, but his main concern was research and teaching. Some of the wartime developments—especially in radar—had opened up entirely new experimental techniques, involving the use of microwaves to study certain extremely subtle phenomena involving atoms. In 1947, for example, the experimental physicist W. E. Lamb and his student R. C. Retherford succeeded in measuring, in a series of experiments that they performed at Columbia University, a tiny shift—known now as the Lamb shift—in the energy levels of the electron in the hydrogen atom. Before the war, a few theoretical physicists had conjectured that such a shift might exist, caused by the interaction of the electron with its radiation field, and there were some experimental hints of its existence as well. The problem was that the shift came out as infinite when it was calculated with the theoretical methods that were then in use. But when Lamb measured it he found that it was finite and very small. In 1955, he was awarded the Nobel Prize in Physics for this work. The work inspired the development of entirely new theoretical methods to compute these effects—a field that is called quantum electrodynamics. In 1947, Bethe produced the first theoretical calculation of the Lamb shift, and immediately thereafter Schwinger, then at Harvard, and Feynman, at Cornell, each created a general theory of quantum electrodynamics. (Some of this work had been done independently in 1943 by Sinitiro Tomonaga, at Tokyo

University, but it became known here only in 1948.) For a time, it appeared that Schwinger and Feynman had produced different theories, but Freeman Dyson, who is now a professor of physics at the Institute for Advanced Study, in Princeton, showed in 1948 that in fact the two methods were equivalent, and he also greatly extended their range of applicability.

Dyson, who was born in England, had been a mathematics prodigy but had decided when he was twenty-two to switch to theoretical physics, which he studied at Cambridge. In 1947, Bethe received a letter of recommendation from the distinguished British mathematical physicist G. I. Taylor, at Cambridge, that read, "I have a student here who is not too bad and maybe you will like him. I am sending him to you since he is interested in changing from mathematics to theoretical physics." Fortunately, Bethe, who had had experience with letters of recommendation from British scientists, realized that this was a strongly positive recommendation. The student was Dyson, whom Bethe regards as the most brilliant student he has ever had.

Chapter 4

The H-Bomb

"IN 1949, not long after the Soviet Union exploded its first atomic device, Teller came to me and said, 'Now we have to do the super,'" Bethe told me. "I was very doubtful. I did not think that this constituted provocation. I thought that, after all, the Russians had got their first explosion at just about the time Seitz and I thought they would—four years after ours—and that we had had to expect it. I also thought that for a long time to come we would have a tremendous superiority in number of nuclear weapons, in sophistication of weapons, and in delivery capacity. I thought that there was no need to develop the super, and that if neither we nor they had a super we would both be better off. However, I was willing to consider it. During the discussion with Teller, my wife came into the room and said to both of us very earnestly, 'You don't want to do this.' She felt that the atomic bomb was bad enough, and that increasing its power a thousand times was simply irresponsible. I was still undecided about what to do.

"In October of 1949, there was a meeting in Princeton of the so-called Emergency Committee of Atomic Scientists, of which Einstein was the official chairman but which was actually directed by Szilard. I took the opportunity offered by this meeting to go to Princeton and talk to people. I remember that I walked into the meeting room and Leo Szilard greeted me by saying, 'Ah, here comes Hans Bethe from Los Alamos.' I protested that I was not at Los Alamos and didn't know if I wanted to go back there. At about this time, Teller and I went to see Oppenheimer at the Institute for Advanced Study. We didn't know where he stood on the super, and it did not become clear to me at that meeting. But he did show us a letter from James Conant"—then president of Harvard. "Conant said that the H-bomb project would go ahead only over his dead body. Oppenheimer just read us the letter—he didn't argue against a crash program himself. In my decision not to return to Los Alamos, I was persuaded not by Oppenheimer but by my wife and by Weisskopf and Placzek." V. F. Weisskopf and Georg Placzek, recent refugee physicists from Europe, had both played important roles in the Theoretical Division at Los Alamos, and both opposed the crash program to build the super. "Weisskopf vividly described to me a war with hydrogen bombs—what it would mean to destroy a whole city like New York with one bomb, and how hydrogen bombs would change the military balance by making the attack still more powerful and the defense still less powerful. This is what persuaded me, not the meeting with

Oppenheimer. I have explained this to Teller many times, but he and others still blamed Oppenheimer for my not returning to Los Alamos."

Bethe continued, "A few days later, I told Teller over the phone that I would not join the project. He was disappointed. I felt relieved. Thereafter we waited anxiously for the decision of the General Advisory Committee." This committee, of which Oppenheimer was chairman, had the responsibility of advising the Atomic Energy Commission whether or not to proceed with a crash program to build the super. "We did not know at all how their decision would come out. I was a witness before the committee, and the members asked me what I thought about the technical feasibility of building the super. The chances didn't look good then, but they also did not look bad. The real problems with the design that was then considered, and is now called the classic super, came out only in the summer of 1950, when it was shown that it just wouldn't work. But in the fall of 1949 most of us and most of the members of the committee were convinced that it really wasn't necessary to try to build it. So we were really shocked when President Truman decided in favor of a crash program. About a dozen of us who were members of the American Physical Society spoke out against the H-bomb in response to Truman's decision. We held a press conference, at which we were given a very hard time. I also wrote an article against the super for *Scientific American*, which appeared in the spring of 1950 and was more favorably received. But in the meantime the project was under way at Los Alamos, very much under the guidance of Edward Teller, who had moved from Chicago back to Los Alamos for the purpose."

Bethe spent June of 1950 at Los Alamos—"with the express understanding that I would not do anything for the

H-bomb," he told me. "During this visit, I heard of the calculations that showed that the classic super—Teller's device—would very likely not work. There was a growing feeling that the lab was engaged in a wild-goose chase. Soon, the Korean War broke out, and this pushed me once again into more active participation. But my chief desire was to clinch the argument that the H-bomb would not work. Teller was at that time designing an experiment that had to do with the ignition of the bomb, and the following winter I looked at a few features of it to see if they had been correctly designed. But by January of 1951 there were additional theoretical arguments showing that the classic super would not work."

Bethe continued, "Teller was completely despondent during that period. He was walking around in deep thought and was terribly moody and got into fights with everybody. He had a really hard time. But in February of 1951 he and Ulam"—Stanislaw Ulam, a brilliant Polish-born mathematician who had come to Los Alamos during the war and had remained there—"found a completely new way to make a hydrogen bomb. I used to say that Ulam was the father of the hydrogen bomb and Edward was the mother, because he carried the baby for quite a while. Anyway, with this new idea I was convinced that the thing could be done, and since it could be done we had to be afraid that the Russians could and would do it, too. Previously, when it was so uncertain, I'd thought we might as well not do it, on the assumption that they would not know how to do it, either. But now I became convinced that there was no way of stopping it, and so I was willing to participate. In 1952, partly at Teller's urging and partly at the urging of Norris Bradbury, who had succeeded Oppenheimer as director, I did go to Los Alamos for eight months, from February to September, and participated to a modest extent in the design of the H-bomb—not in much detail but enough to be useful. In retrospect, I am doubtful whether it really was necessary to develop the H-bomb, even after we recognized that it was technically feasible. On this subject, Herbert York, who from 1952 through 1958 was director of the Livermore Laboratory, near Berkeley, and later became director of Defense Research and Engineering—the highest technical job in the Defense Department—and who has now been for many years professor of physics at the San Diego campus of the University of California, has written a very pertinent book, *The Advisors*. In it, he shows, from a careful study of Russian publications, that the Russian hydrogen bomb was ready about three years after ours. It is at least possible that they might not have embarked on the project if we had not done so. But, you may ask, what if they had developed an H-bomb after all? Well, we would surely have known about this at the time they tested the device—an H-bomb test is unmistakable, because of the debris it puts into the air. There would then still have been time for us to follow their lead, and end up with an H-bomb perhaps three years after *them*. In the intervening three years, we would have had a vast superiority in ordinary atomic bombs, so there would really have been no danger to our security."

I asked Bethe if after the twenty-eight years since Ulam and Teller had had their idea there was still reason to keep it secret.

"Yes," Bethe said. "It is not an obvious idea. It took the French ten years to find it, and their scientists are not stupid. Somehow, the Chinese got it awfully fast. We don't understand how. But if it took the French ten years, then it will take a new country with fewer and less competent scientists much longer than that, so it seems to me that keeping the secret is very much worthwhile."

Surprisingly, when Teller's design for the hydrogen bomb had been accepted, he left Los Alamos and returned to Chicago. Feeling that the hydrogen bomb was being built by the wrong people, he agitated for the construction of another laboratory. "In 1952, Teller got his laboratory"—Livermore—"while the bomb was being built at Los Alamos," Bethe said. "In the fall of 1952, there was a brief attempt to delay or cancel the test of the hydrogen bomb. The idea was that the United States might announce that we had the bomb ready for testing but would refrain from testing it as long as the Russians did the same. In the absence of testing, neither side would have put hydrogen weapons into its arsenal; their design is much too complicated to be relied on without a test. The security of all countries would be greatly enhanced if no country had H-bombs. But in fact the test was made in 1952, the Russians tested their H-bomb three years later, and now five countries have tested hydrogen weapons"—the three others being Britain, France, and China.

On December 3, 1953, President Eisenhower, acting through Lewis Strauss, the chairman of the Atomic Energy Commission, ordered a "blank wall" to be placed between Oppenheimer and any classified material, because of allegations that he was a security risk. The absurdity of this was captured in a Herblock cartoon that showed Oppenheimer on one side of a wall and Strauss on the other side with Eisenhower, and had an Uncle Sam figure examining this strange scene and asking, "Who's being walled off from what?" On December 23rd, Oppenheimer was presented with a formal letter of charges, some of which had to do with his attitude toward the construction of the hydrogen bomb. Bethe heard about these proceedings for the first time when the A.E.C. bill of particulars was made public, along with Oppenheimer's reply.

"The particulars came as a total surprise to me," he said. "I had suspected that he might get into trouble over his attitude toward the hydrogen bomb, but that he was termed a security risk went far beyond anything that could have been expected. Actually, the charge of disloyalty because of his initial opposition to the development of the hydrogen bomb was ultimately dismissed by the hearing board, which was chaired by Gordon Gray, then president of the University of North Carolina. But I had known nothing about the other allegations, which concerned his early associations with Communists. The main point in the A.E.C.'s bill of particulars was that in 1943 Oppenheimer lied to Army Intelligence officers in order to shield a friend, Haakon Chevalier, and that therefore Oppenheimer could not be trusted. On this point, the Gray Board sustained the allegations, and so did the A.E.C., in rejecting Oppenheimer's appeal against the Gray Board's decision, thus revoking Oppenheimer's clearance—or, rather, refusing to reinstate it. All the allegations had been well known to the A.E.C. for many years prior to the hearings and had been reviewed a number of times. Oppenheimer's clearance had always been sustained. But because of Senator Joseph McCarthy's activities, 1953 was a very difficult time. Some of my colleagues were presented in a bad light because of things they had done in the thirties. Having seen what had happened in Germany, I was not at all sure how far McCarthyism would go. It might well have led to the persecution of liberals in general, with no Communist association needed."

Soon after the charges were published, there was a physics conference in Rochester, which Oppenheimer and Bethe both attended. "At this conference, Oppie told me that he had decided to go through with the security hearings—that he couldn't just quietly resign after all that had happened," Bethe told me. " 'But,' he said, 'no matter what happens during the hearings, the Atomic Energy Commission cannot do anything but find me guilty.' He was absolutely right. In the existing political atmosphere, there could be no other outcome."

On April 12, 1954, the hearings conducted by the Gray Board on behalf of the Atomic Energy Commission began, and on April 28th Teller was a witness against Oppenheimer. Shortly before Teller was to testify, Bethe and his wife went to see him. "I tried to persuade him to testify in favor of Oppie—or, at least, not against him," Bethe recalled. "Most of Teller's arguments against Oppie involved questions of judgment on which the two of them had differed, and were, in my view, no basis for conducting a security hearing. But Teller was immovable."

Most of the scientific community was outraged not only at the fact that Teller testified but also at the form his testimony took. Whatever his intentions may have been, his testimony appeared to many people to have a calculated ambiguity, whose effect was devastating. He was questioned by Roger Robb, the attorney for the Gray Board.

Robb asked, "To simplify the issues here, let me ask you this question: Is it your intention, in anything that you are about to testify to, to suggest that Dr. Oppenheimer is disloyal to the United States?"

"I do not want to suggest anything of the kind," Teller said. "I know Oppenheimer as an intellectually most alert and a very complicated person, and I think it would be presumptuous and wrong on my part if I would try in any way to analyze his motives. But I have always assumed, and I now assume, that he is loyal to the United States. I believe this, and I shall believe it until I see very conclusive proof to the opposite."

Robb then said, "Now a question which is the corollary of that. Do you or do you not believe that Dr. Oppenheimer is a security risk?"

"In a great number of instances I have seen Dr. Oppenheimer act—I understood that Dr. Oppenheimer acted—in a way which for me was exceedingly hard to understand," Teller replied. "I thoroughly disagreed with him in numerous issues, and his actions frankly appeared to me confused and complicated. To this extent, I feel that I would like to see the vital interests of this country in hands which I understand better and therefore trust more. In this very limited sense, I would like to express a feeling that I would feel personally more secure if public matters would rest in other hands."

Later, Chairman Gray asked, "Do you feel that it would endanger the common defense and security to grant clearance to Dr. Oppenheimer?"

Teller answered, "I believe . . . that Dr. Oppenheimer's character is such that he would not knowingly and willingly do anything that is designed to endanger the safety of this country. To the extent, therefore, that your question is directed toward intent, I would say I do not see any reason to deny clearance." He added, "If it is a question of wisdom and judgment as demonstrated by actions since 1945, then I would say one would be wiser not to grant clearance."

After this exchange, a remarkable scene took place in the hearing room. Teller went over to Oppenheimer, shook his hand, and said, "I'm sorry."

Oppenheimer replied, "After what you've just said, I don't understand what you mean."

In the end, Oppenheimer lost his clearance, and Teller lost most of his former friends and associates in the physics community.

"I did not see Teller for a long time after this, and our relationship was strained from then on," Bethe told me. "We still encountered each other from time to time, and we were not unfriendly outwardly, but we never discussed this event. There was no question where I stood, however. Only in the last five years have things changed again. The issues of the fifties and sixties, which had separated us, have lost their urgency, and other issues have taken their place. In this changed atmosphere, Teller and I are friends again, although not with the intimacy of the old days."

Oppenheimer died in 1967, and at his funeral Bethe delivered a memorial address in which he said, "It took until April, 1962, before the government made amends. Then President Kennedy invited him to a White House dinner for Nobel Prize winners. And in 1963, just after taking office, President Johnson presented to Oppenheimer the highest honor given by the A.E.C., the fifty-thousand-dollar Enrico Fermi Award. In his acceptance remarks, Oppenheimer said, 'I think it is just possible, Mr. President, that it has taken some charity and some courage for you to make this award today.' Oppenheimer took the outcome of the security hearing very quietly, but he was a changed person; much of his previous spirit and liveliness had left him. Excluded from government work, he apparently did not have the strength to return to active work in physics."

Before the Second World War, Bethe's only interest had been in doing research in pure science. His war work had taught him that applying the results of research could be as challenging as investigating the fundamental laws of physics. Therefore, when he was asked to serve as a consultant to industries, he was willing to spend a great deal of effort on problems of application. At first, these were mostly related to the peaceful use of atomic energy. He served as a consultant to three industrial laboratories and one laboratory of the Atomic Energy Commission on the design of two different types of nuclear reactor to be used for the production of power. Though he did not get involved with the engineering details, he became familiar with many of the engineering problems in reactor design. His main concern was predicting the behavior of power reactors in operation under various conditions. He was especially concerned about reactor safety, and in 1949 he wrote the first paper on the safety of the so-called fast-breeder reactor— the fuel-breeding reactor that is now coming into use abroad. This is a subject he has continued to work on over the years.

In the nineteen-fifties, Bethe began branching out into other fields of applied science. "I find it most helpful to work on a variety of problems," he told me. "The methods that I learned in reactor work have helped me in working on lasers, and the knowledge I gained from working on rockets has been useful in some of the work I have been doing recently in astrophysics. One of the strengths I have is that in my work as a consultant I can make use of a large number of different mathematical and physical techniques and can teach them to the people who work with me."

Bethe's most enduring work in applied physics began in 1955 and was stimulated by Teller's student Arthur Kantrowitz. Kantrowitz was then a professor of aeronautical engineering at Cornell, and in the course of a conversation he happened to have with Victor Emanuel, who was

both a trustee of Cornell and the chairman of the board of
the Avco Manufacturing Corporation, Emanuel pointed out
that no one knew how to design a rocket that could reenter
the atmosphere without burning up. Kantrowitz said that
if Emanuel would furnish him with a small laboratory he
could solve the problem. According to Bethe, one of
Kantrowitz's mottoes is that in scientific and engineering
problems one should pick only those problems over which
one has an "unfair advantage." In this case, Kantrowitz's
unfair advantage was that he knew how to duplicate in an
inexpensive laboratory the conditions that a rocket encounters when it reenters the atmosphere. Up to that time,
the generally accepted notion had been that the only way
to test a rocket's behavior at reentry was to fire one
above the atmosphere and see what happened—a very expensive procedure. Kantrowitz knew how to use shock
waves to drive the air in a shock tube past a model nose
cone at velocities comparable to the ones that would be
encountered in reentry. A shock tube costs a few thousand dollars, while testing a missile can cost a few hundred
million. Thus, the Avco Everett Laboratory was set up for
Kantrowitz and a dozen students and former students, and
Bethe was brought in as a consultant.

Until Kantrowitz attacked the problem, scientists had
believed that to reenter the atmosphere successfully a nose
cone would have to be polished to an incredible degree of
accuracy. As Bethe recalls it, the accuracies that were being
discussed were one part in ten million on a vehicle a few
feet in diameter. "It was a crazy scheme, and it would
not have worked anyway," he said. The first idea that the
Kantrowitz group exploited was to use a fairly blunt metal
nose cone, which would be cooled by having a liquid flowing behind the metal when the nose cone moved through

the atmosphere at high speeds. The air just in front of a cone reentering the atmosphere is heated to such high temperatures that it begins to glow, and some of this radiated light falls back on the cone and heats it up further. "From my Los Alamos days, I knew something about how air radiates," Bethe explained. "We had studied that problem in connection with how a fireball develops around an exploding atomic bomb."

The blunt-nose-cone design had the disadvantage of working only if the nose cone reentered at a relatively low speed. "At this point, Wernher von Braun came to the rescue," Bethe said. "He had designed the reentry vehicles for space flight and for the first medium-range missiles. His idea was to use an ablating cover—an outer skin that would gradually melt or evaporate as heat was transferred to it. But, being a pure engineer, he had never gone into the theory of why ablation works and what it depends on. That is what we got into at Avco Everett. Most ablating surfaces are glassy substances. Glass will melt at a certain temperature, and as it gradually becomes a liquid it loses its viscosity. I developed a theory of how glass would flow when it was heated up to two or three thousand degrees Celsius. It turned out that the surface layer of the glass would flow very little, so it could take up the heat of reentry without flowing away, and thereby protect the nose cone. The exact substance that is put on nose cones is a terrible mess, and the formula is, as far as I know, still classified. It's some very complicated mixture of an organic substance with a glassy substance. When it came to the actual choice of materials, I just listened to what the engineers wanted to put in and deferred to their judgment, merely telling them what material properties to look for."

In 1956, Bethe was appointed to the President's Science

Advisory Committee, or P.S.A.C., which had been established in 1951 and later became an advisory body for the President's special science adviser. The first special assistant for science and technology—James Killian, the president of M.I.T.—was appointed by Eisenhower in 1957, and in 1959 Killian was succeeded by George Kistiakowsky, the Harvard chemist who had played a crucial role in designing the explosives system that ignited the first atomic bombs. In 1973, President Nixon dismantled the P.S.A.C., but today there is again a science adviser to the President—the geologist Frank Press. Because of his work on rockets, Bethe became a member of a P.S.A.C. subcommittee that was to study the possibility of developing an anti-ballistic missile. Here he found himself in the position of a chess player who is asked to play against himself, since he was also engaged in designing decoy techniques to make missiles more difficult to shoot down. In particular, he participated in the development of some of the "chaff packages" that are released in enormous quantities by reentering rockets to prevent an incoming missile from being detected by radar. This work convinced him and the other members of the subcommittee that the development of a realistic antiballistic-missile system was essentially hopeless. It was, they found, so much easier and so much more economical to improve the offensive capabilities of missiles than to defend against them by trying to shoot them down that the deployment of an ABM system was a misleading waste of money. "Each year, our subcommittee recommended that the Pentagon not deploy an ABM, and when Secretary of Defense Robert McNamara came into office, in 1961, he seemed to agree with us," Bethe recalled. "Things went along like this until 1967, when President Johnson and Secretary McNamara suddenly decided to deploy the ABM. McNamara's memorandum struck us as very strange—as if he had been reluctant to write it. For the first eighty percent of it, he repeated all the arguments that he had been given against deploying the system, and then he suddenly turned around and said that now we would deploy an ABM system. He admitted that such a system would never work against the Russians, but said that it might work against the Chinese—who at that time did not have any intercontinental ballistic missiles."

Soon after this decision was made, McNamara resigned. As the public debate over the proposed ABM system continued, Bethe and his colleague Richard Garwin, of the I.B.M. Watson Research Center and Columbia University, wrote an influential article for *Scientific American* in which they argued that such a system would not work at all as a means of defending a large area but that it *might* work in defending a certain point, such as a missile site. They thought, however, that even this point defense did not make much sense. Any ABM system, they reasoned, can be defeated if the attacker increases the number of his offensive missiles sufficiently—and this can be done at a cost less than that of the ABM system itself. Furthermore, the attacker, to be "on the safe side," would very likely add more missiles to his force than would actually be necessary simply to overwhelm the ABM. So in the end the country that has deployed an ABM system is even less secure than it was before.

The Nixon Administration took over a modification of President Johnson's ABM program under which only Minuteman-missile sites were to be defended. The program was passed by the Senate in 1969. The Russians, who had started to deploy such a system around Moscow, had also become convinced that it didn't make much sense. In the first SALT talks, both sides agreed to limit the deployment of ABMs to such a low level that they did not defend against anything. Today, the Russians have stopped the deployment, and the United States has dismantled its system altogether. The amount of money that was wasted on this exercise is staggering.

Meanwhile, Bethe had been taking part in what has turned out to be a partly successful attempt to ban tests of atomic weapons, and this activity once again brought him into direct conflict with Teller. "In the long run, we were somewhat instrumental in having the Arms Control and Disarmament Agency created, under Kennedy," Bethe said. "But we began, in 1957, by asking ourselves, 'What can we do about arms control?' I suggested that one thing we could do would be to have a ban on nuclear-weapons tests, and we discussed what such a ban would accomplish and what it would not accomplish. Up to that time, essentially all the tests had been above-ground. I had been the chairman of another committee, which analyzed the results of the United States' monitoring of Russian tests. Therefore, I knew something about the detection of atomic tests. James Killian, the science adviser, went to see Eisenhower to ask him if he would be interested in having us investigate the question of a possible nuclear-test ban and what its effects might be. He was interested; and I was made chairman of that committee. We had members from the Atomic Energy Commission, the Defense Department, the Central Intelligence Agency, the weapons laboratories, and the State Department. The people from the State Department favored a test ban, for political reasons. The Defense Department was against it; the Atomic Energy Commission was sort of neutral; Teller's laboratory at Livermore was strongly against it; Los Alamos was for it; and then I myself was for it. We quickly decided that it would make some difference to our atomic-weapons program if we could not carry out the next series of nuclear-weapons tests, which was planned for the spring and summer of 1958, but that we could probably afford to stop testing after that series. We also decided that such a ban would make much more of a difference to the Russians, because at the time they were not as far advanced as we were in thermonuclear weapons. To me, this was a very strong argument in favor of a test ban. If we had an advantage and could freeze it and the Russians wanted a test ban, why not have it?"

Bethe continued, "We next took up the matter of how to detect tests. We all agreed that we could detect atmospheric tests quite easily, and the detecting devices existed that might make it even easier to detect tests in the ocean. But then the Livermore people said that testing could be done underground—in fact, such testing had been done, once. What, they asked, were we going to do about that? We had some seismologists in our group, and they pointed out that there would be a seismic signal and that there were certain criteria by which one could distinguish an underground atomic explosion from the signals given off by earthquakes. Such detection was less certain than the detection of tests in other media, but we agreed that we could monitor at least the big underground tests by the seismic method. Just at this time, space flight was coming in, and soon Edward Teller claimed that in the future people would do tests in space—for example, behind the moon. Well, we put all this in a report of sixty pages, which was submitted to the President. I presented it at a National Security Council meeting, and Eisenhower was quite interested. I had lots of charts that had been made by the committee staff for me to use at the meeting, and all sorts of generals were present, along with Cabinet officers. The only questions were from the Secretary of State, John Foster Dulles. He was fundamentally in favor of a test ban, but he asked some very searching questions. Most of the others listened to the report in stony silence, and then I was dismissed.

"Soon after that, Khrushchev wrote an open letter to Eisenhower proposing that all nuclear-weapons tests be stopped. The letter was cleverly timed to arrive just before our planned long series of tests in the spring and summer of 1958. These had been well prepared, and it would be to the Russians' advantage if we did not carry them out. The Russians were testing continually, but we tested big H-bombs only every two years, so to stop testing just before our series was scheduled would be an advantage to them, and to stop just after our series would be an advantage to us. Eisenhower rejected Khrushchev's initiative, but he did suggest that a conference of experts from the two sides be held to determine to what degree we and the Russians could detect each other's tests. This was held in July and August of 1958. I was not a delegate—Lewis Strauss saw to that—but I was there as a technical expert. We made our presentations of detection methods, and the Russians made theirs. It turned out that they had developed pretty much the same system of detection for our tests that we had developed for theirs. I was asked to present our system for detecting tests in space, and I started by talking about satellites. There was some consternation at first, because the Russians thought I might be referring to the Polish and Rumanian delegates to the conference. But once the Russians understood, they were very enthusiastic about the use of satellite systems, which they had also thought of.

II / Working on the Bomb

Finally, the whole group—the United States, Britain, Russia, and several more countries on both sides—reached an agreement on what strength of explosions we could detect under what circumstances. Eisenhower liked it, but he almost never decided anything directly, so he appointed another committee, called the Committee of Principals. This committee didn't get anywhere, because its members couldn't agree: the science adviser, who by then was Kistiakowsky, and the Secretary of State were for the test ban, while the A.E.C. and the Pentagon people were against it. Allen Dulles, the head of the C.I.A., was for it one day and against it the next. Meanwhile, Eisenhower and Khrushchev decided to hold a diplomatic conference on the test ban.

"This foot-dragging gave Teller an opportunity to initiate all sorts of efforts to torpedo the whole thing. His most effective tactic was launching the idea of testing in a big hole. He said that the Russians could dig a big hole below ground—an enormous cavity—and if the explosion inside was sufficiently small the signal coming from it would be greatly attenuated. The notion was pretty fantastic, but it swept the newspapers and it swept the government—especially the Joint Congressional Committee on Atomic Energy. I testified before Representative Chet Holifield, of California. He was absolutely against stopping weapons tests, and most of the witnesses his committee invited were against it. Teller appeared and came on terribly strong. I had a very unpleasant hearing before the committee. I was on the defensive, because the cards were stacked against me. And I made a mistake—I said we'd make it all work by putting a large number of unmanned stations in Russia. That got into the New York *Times*, which really tore me to pieces. The episode was a very unhappy one. Anyway,

Eisenhower, for once, had taken the bull by the horns and proposed a *limited* test ban. He proposed that all atmospheric tests and marine tests be banned, along with all underground tests above a certain strength. The limit was about twenty kilotons, and such a ban would have been very good. But he also wanted some on-site inspections in Russia. It was decided that sixty inspections per year were needed to investigate seismic signals that might be interpreted as due to either nuclear explosions or earthquakes. The Russians turned this proposal down and offered three inspections, which was actually quite a concession for them. We made a counterproposal of seven, but the negotiations were broken off. I decided to write an article —it appeared in *The Atlantic Monthly* for August, 1960— explaining my position on the test ban and pointing out that it didn't really matter if the Russians could cheat a little bit on the underground tests, since any test in which they could cheat would be only a rather small explosion. I also explained that at that time we had an advantage in nuclear weapons but that if both sides continued to test, this advantage would disappear, and that the whole point of the test ban was to use it as a first step toward more general arms control. My article was reprinted in the so-called Headline Series, which is a series of pamphlets for use in high schools, and right next to it was an article by Teller, in which he took the opposite view on each point. These articles were widely read. Since that time, all sorts of improved methods of detecting tests have been developed. We did launch several satellites to detect clandestine explosions in outer space. They never detected any, but they did find out all sorts of marvellous things about the earth's magnetic field and about the solar wind of particles coming to the earth. Finally, in 1963, a limited test ban was signed—much more limited than Eisenhower had intended, because in the new treaty underground tests of any size were allowed. But tests in the atmosphere were forbidden. This was signed by us, the Russians, and the British. The French, though they did not sign it, have recently given up their atmospheric tests. However, if you allow testing underground, unless the allowed yield is very low—say, ten kilotons or less—you are not doing much for arms control. A few years ago, we concluded a ban on underground tests of a hundred and fifty kilotons or more, which clearly means very little from the point of view of arms control. By now, we have just about all the weapons anybody can possibly think of."

PART III

Prophet of Energy

Chapter 5

The Problem

Bethe formally retired from Cornell in the summer of 1975. This does not seem to have changed his life a great deal. His office at the university, where he spends his time when he is not lecturing or consulting elsewhere, is piled high with books, manuscripts, letters, and articles that people all over the world send him in order to get his views on them. Today—as he has done for much of his life—Bethe devotes much of his time to looking carefully at numbers. His memory is prodigious, and he has the ability—unusual even among physicists—to hold in his mind all the strands of the most complicated technical arguments imaginable, and, further, to manipulate them, and to come up with reasonable estimates of the consequences of their development. Thanks to this ability, he has worked successfully on a broader range of technical problems than almost any other modern theoretical physicist. Enrico Fermi had a similar range, as did Bethe's first great teacher, Arnold Sommerfeld. Since 1974—the year of the Arab oil embargo—Bethe has been devoting nearly all his time to the study of the energy problem. Where do we stand, and where are we going? Where can we go?

The concern and the intensity that Bethe brings to the problem reflect experiences from his childhood. President Carter has declared that this country should regard the energy crisis as "the moral equivalent of war," but the President and most of the rest of us do not have firsthand knowledge of what such a crisis can do to the population of an industrialized society. Bethe has. He was just entering his teens when the First World War ended, and his memories of its aftermath in Germany have never left him. As he recalls it, "One of my important teenage experiences was the great German inflation. It was terrible. In the years just after the war—1919 to 1922—the value of the German mark went down by a factor of about a thousand, and in 1923 this was topped by a further inflation of a factor of a *billion*. My father, who headed the Physiology Department at the University of Frankfurt, got his salary twice a week to keep pace with the continuing devaluation. I was the only person in the family who could at least deal with the numbers and grasp the fact that a million of today's marks were worth only five hundred thousand of yesterday's. So it was my job to collect my father's salary and spend it as quickly as I could. The money was generally paid by the university cashier at ten o'clock in the morning. By one o'clock the money had to be spent, because the stores closed between one and two. The new dollar value of the mark would be published during this hour, and in the afternoon everything would be twice as expensive as it had been in the morning—or, sometimes, only one and a half times. Fortunately, I didn't have school in the morning—only in the afternoon—so I would go twice a week on my bicycle to get the money and spend it immediately. I had a list of the food items I was to buy, and after I returned home with the food the family had something to eat for the next few days."

Bethe continued, "The reason I did not have school in the morning was that there was a scarcity of coal, and the scarcity of coal was due, in turn, to the occupation of the Ruhr district by the French in retaliation for nonpayment of war reparations by the Germans. The Ruhr was the main source of coal, so there was a shortage all over Germany at that time. Schools consolidated. Our school was combined with another school, whose students had their instruction in the morning, while we had ours in the afternoon. I witnessed the complete breakdown of the monetary system and the partial breakdown of coal supplies and food supplies which went with it. The whole period from the end of the war, in 1918, until the beginning of 1924 was a time of tremendous insecurity—insecurity in the industrial base of Germany and in the supply of goods. I am afraid that unless we solve our energy problems something similar may happen here and elsewhere in the future."

Until recently, the energy debate in this country was conducted in an almost surreal atmosphere. We appeared to be awash in oil and gasoline, and most Americans seemed to feel that this state of affairs would continue indefinitely. The crisis in Iran and the rise in the price of oil on the world market may have changed that. For the first time, the American people are apparently beginning to come to grips with what is going to be a fact of life for many years —we are going to be desperately in need of useful energy sources. The purely technical problem of developing new sources is compounded by the fact that we live in an age when few of us truly understand how anything works. Technology has got away from us, and intelligent citizens find it increasingly difficult to make the decisions necessary to safeguard the future of us all. The difficulty is compounded when scientists and engineers disagree among themselves. Furthermore, we *are* dealing in futuristic estimates on which, within certain limits, honest and informed people may disagree. What is essential is to develop a sense of these limits and a general feeling for what is true and what is not.

For these reasons, Bethe's ideas about the energy crisis are particularly valuable. He has often said that he is a pure pragmatist, with no doctrinaire axe to grind. Since he is able to manipulate all the technical concepts involved, talking with him about energy is rather different from the usual discussions of the subject. One is able to say to him, for example, "So-and-So claims that what you think is x is really $2x$. What do you make of that?" Bethe will then patiently explain the consequences if his number is the correct one and the consequences if the other number is correct, and what the consequences would be if the truth lay somewhere in between. He will also explain all the assumptions that have gone into the computation of the various numbers and point out where any of these assumptions, including his own, might be suspect. It is an education both in the subject of energy and in how to think about it.

By definition, miracles do not often happen, and it is not likely that the energy problem will be solved by a miracle.

5 / *The Problem*

The solution, if there is one, will be found in the laws of physics. Physicists identify four basic forces in nature. In order of increasing strength, they are: the force of gravity; the so-called weak force; the electromagnetic force; the so-called strong force. Gravity is the weakest force; its apparent strength in holding us to the surface of the earth is due to the fact that we and the earth are made up of a vast number of gravitating masses, whose effects add up. The weak force is responsible for processes like the radioactive decay of many nuclei, and also for some of the energy-generating processes in stars like the sun. The electromagnetic force produces not only the evident effects of electricity and magnetism but also chemical reactions. The strong force holds the nucleus of an atom together, despite the fact that the protons in a nucleus, which are positively charged particles, tend to repel one another electrically.

The interactions among these forces do not produce energy but, rather, conserve it. In fact, the term "energy production" is a misnomer, for no force or combination of forces produces energy. There are different types of energy, and the interactions among the four basic forces transform one type of energy into another; the total remains constant. Consider the water flowing in a mountain stream. The stream's energy is a result of gravitation; the force of gravity pulls the stream along, and some of the potential energy of gravitation is converted into the energy of motion—kinetic energy. This can be converted into electrical energy if we use the moving water to turn an electrical generator. The water in the stream has been produced by the melting of snow, and the melting has been caused by the snow's absorption of the radiant energy of the sun—absorption that involves the electromagnetic force. And the radiant energy of the sun is a result of nuclear fusion. In the sun, fusion is a two-step process. First, the weak force causes two free hydrogen protons in the sun's interior to fuse, the result being a nucleus of heavy hydrogen, a positron, and a neutrino. These three particles have less mass than the two protons, and the loss of mass is available as kinetic energy, shared among the three particles. Then the electromagnetic force causes the heavy-hydrogen nucleus—known as a deuteron, because it consists of two particles, a neutron and a proton—to fuse with another proton, the result of this fusion being a light isotope of helium and a gamma ray, which is a quantum of electromagnetic energy. The gamma ray diffuses out of the sun's interior, gradually changing its wave-length to that of ordinary light, and this light eventually arrives at the surface of the earth.

In the course of energy transformations, "useful" energy is constantly being depleted. Some of the kinetic energy of the mountain stream gets converted into useless heat. Not all the combustion energy of fossil fuels goes into useful work; the remainder, again, is dissipated in useless heat. There is no way to avoid such losses. This is what the Second Law of Thermodynamics has reference to in stating that in any process entropy will normally increase. Entropy is, roughly speaking, a measure of the disorder, or randomness, of a system. The chemical energy stored in a fossil fuel is in a highly ordered state, but when it is converted into the thermal energy of steam—a vapor made up of chaotically moving water molecules—disorder increases. When we use that steam to drive any sort of engine—an electrical generator or a steam locomotive, say—not all the steam's energy can be converted into the ordered motion of the engine; a lot of it remains in the disordered state, and is therefore not useful. It is in this sense that, even though energy is, strictly speaking, conserved at every stage, our energy sources are constantly being depleted.

One thing is therefore certain: a time will come when all the nonrenewable sources of energy on the earth will be gone. The oil and the natural gas will be gone. The uranium will be gone, and so will the coal. To get some sort of feeling for the depletion times involved, Bethe has put together the most accurate estimates of the existing resources and has weighed those estimates against the ways in which we are now using the resources. He has integrated the estimates of commercial enterprises, like oil companies; government estimates, such as those of the United States Geological Survey; and the estimates of various bodies of independent scientists, like the National Academy of Sciences. Where there are differences, he has taken numbers somewhere in the middle. Bethe and many other experts have concluded that until recently, at least, Americans have been using precious nonrenewable resources just about as irresponsibly as they possibly could.

It is instructive to see where the route of such irresponsible use will take us. The first thing we must understand is that if we simply want to maintain our present standard of living, with no improvements, our energy consumption will have to keep increasing in the near future, because our population is increasing. It is true that the birth rate in the United States appears to have levelled off, but this phenomenon is recent, and so for perhaps another decade more people will enter the work force than will retire. Jobs will have to be provided for them. This will require energy, and so will our current goal of bringing into the work force millions of Americans who are now unemployed. There is no sign in our society that any significant group is willing to accept a decrease in its standard of living, and most

III / Prophet of Energy

Americans feel that it is immoral to condemn either their offspring or large sectors of the existing population to permanent unemployment. So energy production, evidently, must be increased. Bethe, in making his analysis, has assumed an annual growth rate of three percent in our gross national product, which, in this case, will have doubled by the year 2000. This is a low growth rate compared to the standards of the fifties and sixties, but it was chosen to give an estimate of our future needs.

The doubling of the gross national product does not automatically mean that twice as much energy will be consumed in the year 2000. In fact, over the past thirty years fuel consumption per unit of G.N.P. has declined very slightly. If strict conservation methods were adopted—and there is not much indication that they will be—then Bethe would accept as the most optimistic serious estimate of our energy needs a forty percent increase over what we now use. To achieve this would mean that we would have to use about a third less energy for everything we make and do.

But suppose we were able to alter our lives. Suppose we could somehow learn to live so that our energy consumption would not increase at all in the next few decades. How would we be able to supply our energy needs in the year 2000? Essentially, everyone who has studied these matters now agrees that, whatever happens, we would not be able to do it with oil. Oil production in the United States peaked in 1970, and we have produced less oil each year since then. (Alaskan oil will only temporarily halt this decline.) As for the great Arabian oil fields, their production will have peaked by the year 2000 or a little later—depending on the rate at which the remaining oil is used. The Soviet Union, which produces about eleven million seven hundred thousand barrels a day—the Saudis currently produce about nine and a half million barrels a day—is also experiencing a production peak, and expects to import oil in the nineteen-eighties. In this country, we now use about six billion barrels of oil a year. Our reserves of discovered oil, including the Alaskan oil, are about sixty billion barrels. If we had to rely on this oil alone, then, it would run out in ten years. The estimates of our undiscovered oil, Bethe finds, range from fifty billion to a hundred and fifty billion barrels; the United States Geological Survey estimates eighty billion. The total supply could be extended another ten years if the methods of recovering oil from wells could be improved by making the oil less viscous. Attempts at reducing the viscosity have been made, with some measure of success. In favorable locations this so-called "tertiary recovery" might be done for twenty-five or thirty dollars a barrel. Nonetheless, it is widely agreed that we will have to continue to import several billion barrels of oil a year.

As the world's reserves of oil diminish, it is becoming clear that sometime before 2000 we will have either to reduce our standard of living dramatically or to find substitutes for oil. With natural gas, the situation seems to be somewhat better; if our supply is used at the present rate, it may last as long as forty years, provided that an all-out effort is made to find new gas and that the effort is successful.

At present, we have operating in this country something like seventy power-producing nuclear reactors, and there are about ninety new ones in various stages of construction. It takes perhaps ten years to build a nuclear power station, and costs a billion dollars. The working lifetime of a station is usually given as thirty years. The fuel for nuclear power stations is a mixture of two uranium isotopes—ninety-seven percent of it being the common isotope U-238, and only three percent the readily fissionable isotope

III / Prophet of Energy

U-235. In the working lifetime of a station, about six thousand tons of uranium ore is used. In order to keep a typical reactor going, fresh fuel must be supplied periodically, and a third of the fuel elements are changed annually. During the three-year period that the fuel normally spends in the reactor, not all the U-235 is fissioned; perhaps a quarter of it is left. Furthermore, in the working cycle of the reactor, plutonium—the fissionable isotope Pu-239—is produced by nuclear reactions in the U-238. In other words, a power reactor regenerates some of its own fuel; something like sixty percent of the used U-235 has been replaced by usable plutonium. Much of this plutonium is itself fissioned while the fuel is in the reactor, yet there is still a substantial amount of fissionable material left in the fuel elements after they have been removed from the reactor—about a third of the original amount. President Carter has decided that we should not reprocess the spent fuel to recover this material, so it is simply being uselessly stored in storage pools adjoining the reactors. The Department of Energy estimates that today there is three and a half million tons of minable uranium oxide in the United States. If this is used in the future as it is being used at present, there is enough to power at least five hundred reactors for thirty years. If five hundred reactors were operating in the year 2000, they would supply about half of our electricity, or a quarter of our total energy needs. But although they would clearly contribute to the solution of our energy problem in the year 2000, they would have no effect a few decades thereafter. Other industrial countries, with less uranium, are not following our example in the use of uranium but are planning to use reactor techniques that "breed" new fuel.

Of coal we have a great deal, but by no means an infinite amount. Estimates of the recoverable coal deposits in this country range between two hundred billion and six hundred billion tons. It has been estimated that in the year 2020 we will have to use something like two and a half billion tons of coal. Most of this will go to make electricity; some will go to make gas and oil; and some will go to make petrochemicals, such as fertilizer. Given the figures, it is quite likely that citizens in the year 2020 will look upon coal much the way we look at oil now. They will feel, rightly, that there is a lot of it, and they will also feel, rightly, that it is a precious, finite resource that may begin to run out at the end of *their* century. For these people, the energy problem will present itself somewhat differently. They will be forced to look at renewable energy sources, and at those alone. To them, the problem may appear as a purely technological one. Can the renewable sources be made to yield the necessary energy? Since these renewable sources—the sun, the oceans, the trees, the wind, the streams—are widely shared by the people of the earth, it is possible to imagine that the international political tensions that dominate our present thinking with respect to the nonrenewable energy sources will have vanished, and that some sort of cooperative global effort will appear to be the most logical way of approaching the harnessing of the renewable ones. In that sense, the next century may turn out to be a good time to be alive—a more benign time. The problem that we have is how to get from here to there without destroying ourselves either by warring over diminishing resources or by polluting our environment beyond repair. None of the choices involved are simple, and none of the paths that we may choose are without risk. What someone like Bethe is able to do is provide an analysis of the various choices and their attendant risks and advantages.

Bethe has remarked that, historically, there has been a time lag of at least twenty years between the invention of a new energy technology and the building of the first prototype. For example, nuclear fission was discovered in 1938, and the first privately financed nuclear power plant in the United States went into operation in Dresden, Illinois, on August 1, 1960. Though some work was done on controlled nuclear fusion in the early fifties, the intense effort to develop it as a power source began only in the late fifties—mostly after the subject was declassified by the United States, on the occasion of the second United Nations International Conference on the Peaceful Uses of Atomic Energy, which took place in Geneva in 1958—and Bethe thinks that the feasibility of fusion power may be proved experimentally in the mid-nineteen-eighties. The reason for such lags is that doing the research and engineering to develop a prototype requires a good deal of time. In addition, building a prototype does not in itself deliver any energy to the consumer, and putting a new technology into extensive use requires a lot of money. The entire Manhattan Project, of which the laboratory at Los Alamos was only one part, cost two billion dollars in the mid-forties, or a present value of about eight billion dollars—eight times the cost of a nuclear power station today. Thus, the nuclear power stations that are being constructed now have a combined cost of a dozen Manhattan Projects. And to put sums of money like this together without dangerously bleeding the economy also requires time—usually a lot more time than the research and development. "Sometimes one hears the suggestion that we should have a Manhattan Project for energy—a concentrated research effort to speed things up," Bethe remarked. "I think that this idea misses the point. While it is true that research and engineering can often be done at an accelerated pace, actually making use of the results to supply a large number of consumers presents a problem of a totally different magnitude. If one adds the time required to engineer the prototype to the time required to put together the vast capital sums for constructing power stations and the time required to build them, then it is fair to say, I think, that any technology that is going to produce substantial energy by the year 2000 has already been invented. This does not mean that improvements in the existing technologies—new inventions related to them—will not be adopted. What it does mean is that only developments related to existing technological ideas are likely to have much of an impact in the next twenty years or so." The existing technologies that are relevant to the energy problem involve the wind, the sun, coal, nuclear fusion, and nuclear fission. Oil and natural gas are omitted from this list because it is not clear that any invention can alter the steady depletion of these resources; so is hydroelectric power, because—in the industrial societies, at least—it is already essentially being fully utilized.

The most controversial of these technologies is surely nuclear fission. Although there are many different types of fission reactor, only one system is in general use for producing commercial electric power. Broadly, that system has two basic components—a reactor and steam generators. In a nuclear power plant, the reactor functions as a heat source; it replaces the coal or oil furnace of a conventional power plant. In so-called pressurized-water reactors—the more common type—this heat is converted into steam in units separate from the reactor; in so-called boiling-water reactors, this conversion to steam takes place within the reactor unit, from which the steam is conducted to the turbines. In either case, once the steam has been produced the electricity is made by entirely conventional methods, with turbines of the sort that are always shown in newspaper photographs when there is a power failure.

In a pressurized-water nuclear power plant, both the reactor and the steam generators are placed inside a building —called the containment building—resembling a large silo, two hundred feet high, of which the reactor occupies a relatively small part. The reactor vessel—a steel chamber whose walls are at least eight inches thick—is about sixteen feet in diameter and about fifty feet high, while the floor of the building has a diameter of about a hundred and twenty-five feet. In this system, water at about five hundred and fifty degrees Fahrenheit is constantly fed into the reactor vessel through large pipes, and is there heated to six hundred and twenty degrees. The heated water is kept under high pressure—about twenty-two hundred and fifty pounds per square inch, as opposed to the normal air pressure of about fifteen pounds per square inch—so that it will not boil. This cycle generates the steam needed to run the turbines and also keeps the reactor core—the fuel within the reactor vessel—at a temperature low enough to prevent its melting. All the potentially serious accidents that pressurized-water reactors are subject to can be traced to some interruption in the cooling cycle.

Where does the fuel in these reactors come from? And what does it cost? Uranium is distributed all over the surface of the earth, at an average concentration of three parts per million; in certain ore deposits, the concentration is as high as thirty percent. In this country, ore with a concentration of a few hundredths of one percent is considered profitable to mine. About ninety-nine and a quarter percent of this uranium is in the form of the isotope U-238, whose nucleus is composed of ninety-two protons and a hundred and forty-six neutrons. The isotope U-235, which has three fewer neutrons, occurs in natural uranium in the ratio of about one part in a hundred and forty. Mined uranium currently costs about forty dollars a pound. After it is mined, this uranium is enriched; that is, it is partly separated into its isotopes until the mixture, instead of being less than one percent U-235, reaches the required three percent—a process that is costly both in energy and in money. When one speaks of reserves of uranium, one means those reserves that can be mined and enriched at a cost low enough to produce energy at rates comparable to those for other fuels. In the future, it may be worthwhile to exploit shale, although it has a much lower concentration of natural uranium, and even to try to recover uranium from seawater, but today these processes are too expensive.

In a conventional power reactor, whether pressurized or boiling, uranium that is chemically bonded to oxygen—uranium oxide—is used. The uranium-oxide fuel is shaped into pellets about an inch long and half an inch in diameter, and these pellets are fitted into tubes about twelve feet long. These tubes, called fuel rods, are made of a zirconium alloy that is highly resistant to radiation damage and will not melt at the working temperature of the reactor. In a large pressurized-water reactor, there are about forty thousand fuel rods, which are packed into bundles of about two hundred rods each. Ordinary water circulates among the fuel rods to cool them.

How does this arrangement generate energy? Part of the natural background radiation, to which we are all subjected, consists of "thermal," or low-energy, neutrons. These neutrons are produced by, for example, cosmic rays entering the earth's atmosphere and breaking up the nuclei of the air. When a thermal neutron encounters a U-235 nucleus, several competitive processes are possible, one of which is that the neutron simply bounces off the uranium. In many of the collisions, however, the thermal neutron will cause the U-235 to split up—to fission—into two lighter nuclei and a number of neutrons. There are at least thirty different ways in which a U-235 nucleus can fission, and in all of them two lighter nuclei emerge, along with a certain number of neutrons. If one averages the number of released neutrons, the figure comes out to about two and a half per fission. Most of the energy that is produced goes into the motion of the fission fragments, giving them their kinetic energy. Since these fragments remain in the fuel rods that contain the uranium pellets, their kinetic energy heats the rods. These rods, in turn, heat the water used for cooling, and so produce the steam that generates the electricity.

How much energy is released in a typical fission? Physicists calculate it in terms of an energy unit called an electron volt, which is, roughly, 4.5×10^{-26} kilowatt-hours— a very small amount of energy on a practical scale. In each fission, about two hundred million electron volts of energy is released. A typical neutron or proton is bound to a uranium nucleus with an energy of about seven million six hundred thousand electron volts, but in the fission fragments the typical binding energy per particle is eight and a half million electron volts. When a substance is transformed into one that is more tightly bound, energy is released. The water molecule, for example, is more tightly bound than the molecules of oxygen and hydrogen, so energy is released when hydrogen burns to form water. Similarly, in a fission the difference in binding energy is released—nearly a million electron volts per nuclear particle—and becomes the kinetic energy of the two fission fragments. Since there are about two hundred nuclear particles in the uranium nucleus, the total energy release per fission is about two hundred million electron volts. The average American uses electric power at a rate of about a thousand watts. A watt is an amount of energy per unit of time; it is an energy rate. A thousand watts—a kilowatt—corresponds to 238.9 calories a second. Since there are about nine thousand hours in a year, the average American uses nearly nine thousand kilowatt-hours of electrical energy in a year. The rest of the world averages about one-fifth of that. If one gram of U-235 could be fissioned completely, it would provide a year's supply of electric power for one American. Even though natural uranium is expensive per pound and separated U-235 even more so, by the early nineteen-seventies the fuel cost of uranium per kilowatt-hour was already less than that of any of the fossil fuels, and projections for 1981 suggest that uranium will cost about one-seventh of what oil will cost and about half as much as coal. Bethe is fond of saying, "Coal is wonderful stuff, but uranium is even better." *

In a reactor, the neutrons released by the U-235 fission are fairly energetic—too energetic to fission more U-235 effectively. The water used for cooling in the reactor emerges in another role—that of "moderator." Collisions

---

* In the technical glossary at the end of the book I have attempted to sort out the rather confusing units in which energy is measured. The numbers that are given in the text are meant to be accurate to about ten percent, so that they are easier to keep in mind. What is called a "barrel" of oil is a quantity of oil that amounts to forty-two gallons. It weighs, incidentally, about two hundred and fifty pounds. If the energy content of this oil, when burned, could be converted into electrical energy without any loss due to efficiency each barrel would yield about seventeen hundred kilowatt-hours. In practice about two-thirds of this energy is lost so that each barrel produces about five hundred kilowatt-hours of electricity when it is used for this purpose. Hence, if all of our electricity were supplied by oil each American would use about eighteen barrels a year for this purpose. As of the year 1978 sixteen percent of our electricity was supplied by oil, forty-five percent by coal, thirteen and one half percent by natural gas, thirteen percent by hydroelectricity, and thirteen percent by nuclear fuels.

with the protons in the water molecules slow the energetic neutrons, and these newly slowed neutrons can, in their turn, fission the U-235. (They can also transform some of the U-238 into Pu-239). That is to say, a chain reaction occurs. Some of the neutrons simply get lost in this process, either by being absorbed into one of the U-238 nuclei or into the oxygen or possible impurities in the water, or by escaping from the reactor altogether by absorption into the steel walls surrounding it. In practice, a reactor must be designed to keep enough neutrons constantly available for further fissions, and if a reactor uses natural uranium —not enriched with U-235—no chain reaction will take place in it unless the moderator is either graphite or heavy water; ordinary water will not work. Because most of the power reactors in use today do use ordinary water for cooling and moderating, they are referred to as light-water reactors.

In the normal working cycle of a light-water power reactor, fission fragments are created each time a U-235 or Pu-239 nucleus undergoes fission. These fission fragments, which are generally unstable nuclei in the middle of the periodic table of elements, collect in the fuel pellets or as gas in the spaces within the fuel rods. Because these fission fragments can capture neutrons, they make the fuel elements unusable by extracting neutrons from the fission chain. Sooner or later, then, the fuel rods have to be removed, and since the present practice is to remove one-third of them annually—if President Carter's program is continued—these fuel rods will simply be stored, with no separation of the still usable uranium and plutonium from the fission fragments. (In volume, something like two cubic metres of waste is present in the removed rods.) Many of the fission fragments have a relatively short half-life, so after a few months or a year of storage much of their radioactivity will have abated. During this time, the rods are put in a pool of water forty feet deep, where they cool off both in temperature and in radioactivity. Nonetheless, because they also contain long-lived radioactive isotopes, provision must be made for storing them over long periods. The long-lived isotopes are of two types: fission fragments such as strontium and cesium, and the so-called actinides, or transuranic elements—the elements into which uranium is transformed—among them plutonium. Strontium and cesium have isotopes with half-lives of about thirty years, and both have biologically unpleasant features, since they are readily absorbed by the human body. Strontium can replace calcium in the bones, and any radioactivity in the bones can lead to cancer. Cesium concentrates in the reproductive system and can cause mutations. These isotopes must be stored in isolation for at least six hundred years—until their radioactivity is reduced to a negligible level. And if the fuel rods are not reprocessed, they will also contain Pu-239, which has a half-life of twenty-four thousand years. Much has been written about the hazards of plutonium. Indeed, it has even been called the most poisonous substance known. It is not. The actual hazard depends on the way in which it gets into the human body. Insoluble plutonium compounds, such as the oxide that would constitute the reactor fuel, if eaten or drunk accidentally would have little effect: nearly all of it would be excreted without being absorbed through the intestinal wall. The danger comes from inhaling plutonium dust. Cancers in the lungs and bones of experimental animals have appeared when the animals have inahled plutonium. Using these experiments as a basis, biologists have set a standard maximum permissible "body burden" of Pu-239 at six micrograms (six millionths of a gram). While no one would wish to be the subject of such exposures there is one well-documented instance when it did occur. During the war, when procedures were much less careful than they are now, twenty-seven machinists and technicians at Los Alamos inhaled plutonium in amounts varying from a quarter to several times the maximal permissible dosage. Twenty-six of these men agreed to participate in a program at Los Alamos in which they would be systematically checked for signs of cancer. Now, more than thirty years later, none of them have developed any illness that could be correlated to their exposure to plutonium. As a group they had inhaled about forty times the maximum permissible amount. This indicates that the present dosage standard has been set conservatively. Plutonium that is stored underground can only migrate back to the surface by the motion of ground water, and hence not in the form of dust, so that even if this should happen it would not pose a grave hazard. Nonetheless, no one wants *any* of this material ever to reenter the biosphere. Thus, its safe storage, along with the other radioactive wastes, remains one of the main concerns of the nuclear-energy program.

The present proposed method of long-term storage calls for the fusing of a number of fuel rods with a ceramic to make a solid package about a foot in diameter. (Recent work done at the Vitreous State Laboratory at Catholic University suggests that a low-impurity, high-silica porous glass is a better matrix for holding these fission fragments than the ceramics. This material, the researchers state, has a durability of many thousands of years.) These packages are then to be put in steel cylinders about fifteen feet long, which are to be permanently stored two thousand feet underground. The preferred storage medium is bedded salt.

An underground bedded-salt deposit has three advantages. First, it is in a region that is free of underground water (if water had been present, it would have dissolved the salt), and water transport is the only important way in which underground deposits can be brought back to the surface of the earth. Second, bedded-salt deposits are in geologically quiet regions—regions that have not had seismic activity in many millions of years, and are thought unlikely to be disturbed by seismic activity in the future. Finally, salt flows plastically under pressure, so any cracks that might be opened up in the salt by mechanical or thermal stress will anneal themselves. (Salt is not the only possible disposal medium; experts agree that granite might be equally good, or possibly even better.) What is proposed is that a mine two thousand feet deep be dug into a salt bed and that tunnels, each just large enough to hold a single cylinder, be dug in the walls of the mine. One such bed has been proposed on federal land in southeastern New Mexico, and this has met with President Carter's approval. However, this site will, it seems, be used only for storing wastes from military applications of nuclear reactors. Waste disposal for civilian power reactors is still in a sort of political limbo.

This situation is typical of the crisis of confidence that has troubled the nuclear-technology program. A large segment of our population has lost faith in technology and technological estimates. Although we do accept hundreds of technological assumptions each day of our lives—that bridges will not collapse when we go over them, that the wheels of our automobiles will not fall off when we drive, that airplanes are safe enough for us to fly in—most of us are in no position to verify the details of such technologies. We must at some point take the word of experts that these things will really work the way they are supposed to. But so much emotion has been engendered in the debate over nuclear energy that many people have lost confidence in any sort of technical expertise in the matter. The fact that the best scientists available have studied the problem does not inspire confidence; rather, it often generates further skepticism. On the positive side, this skeptical attitude has made many of the studies much better and more careful, but skepticism could also bring the nuclear program to an end. Though this might be a source of satisfaction to some, it would have serious consequences. Unless we can come up with realistic alternatives to the known methods of energy production, we will simply have less energy and a drastically lower standard of living—and this, in turn, could have dire social and political consequences.

With respect to waste disposal, it may not seem reasonable to have confidence that a disposal site will remain geologically undisturbed for thousands of centuries, but Bethe points out that nature has provided us with a site where this has already happened. A few years ago, the remains of a "natural" nuclear reactor were discovered in Gabon, in an area that has rich uranium ore, with concentrations of between twenty and thirty percent. Both U-238 and U-235 are radioactive, but U-238 has a longer half-life—which is why it is now so much more abundant than U-235. A billion eight hundred million years ago, however, uranium ore was about three percent U-235. In addition, the ore contained water, which acted as a moderator. This configuration was analogous to the basic design of a light-water reactor and, indeed, it functioned that way. The effect of this "reactor" activity was to leave in the ground an anomalously low concentration of U-235, along with the fission fragments. By analyzing samples of the soil, French radiochemists have found that most of the fission fragments have scarcely moved in the nearly two billion years since they were formed. (The position of the short-lived fragments can be determined by identifying their decay products.) This is also true of the plutonium that the "reactor" generated. It moved less than one millimetre from the time of its formation. Thus, this natural reactor, so long quiescent, provides a model for a disposal site. Meanwhile, until the government sees fit to act, the nuclear power plants operating in this country are disposing of their partly spent fuel by putting the fuel rods in the water pools, which were intended to hold them only temporarily. Since the pools were designed with the idea that there would be a continual turnover in spent fuel rods, which were to be sent elsewhere for reprocessing within a year, their capacity is limited, and the utilities that operate the nuclear plants will soon find themselves in the position of having to construct new pools or to install new racks in the old ones, all of which may turn out to be useless if the government's policy changes.

The widespread concern over the safety of the nuclear-energy program was made agonizingly acute by the accident last March at the Three Mile Island nuclear generating station, near Harrisburg, Pennsylvania. Nuclear power plants at present generate about fifty thousand megawatts of electric power in the United States—almost fourteen prcent of the total. Their operation represents over five hundred reactor-years of experience. Whether one considers this a large or a small amount of experience with commercial power-generating reactors depends on one's estimate of the likelihood that something will go seriously wrong. It is Bethe's view that "one cannot make a reactor safe without having reactors and gaining experience from them." He says, "One can put in many sorts of safety measures, and this has been done, but then one must find out what happens in the real world. There one has to expect some incidents, some anomalous occurrences, and, indeed, some accidents. There are hundreds of occurrences every year. All of them have to be reported to the Nuclear Regulatory Commission. The overwhelming majority of them do not endanger the integrity of the reactor, but they all have to be learned about, because one has to find out what not to do."

The sort of accident that everybody agrees must be avoided at all costs is the one that disrupts the cooling system—the system that keeps the reactor core at a safe temperature. In the light-water power reactors being used today, the cooling system keeps water circulating around the fuel rods. If the flow of water is interrupted and nothing replaces it, the core will melt, and in certain circumstances the melting could lead to a release of radioactivity from the containment building.

All reactors are designed with safeguards. Suspended above the core when the reactor is in operation is a cluster of control rods—thirty-foot-long rods made of neutron-absorbing materials, like boron. When the control rods are lowered into the core, they absorb neutrons and bring the chain-reaction cycle to a halt. In an emergency, the control rods are driven into the core automatically and very rapidly—a procedure known as a scram. (In the boiling-water reactors the safety rods are driven into the core in an emergency. In the more common pressurized reactors these rods are suspended above the core and fall into it in about a second in case of an emergency.) This is the first line of defense. But if the scram fails to operate, the reactor will tend to shut itself off anyway, because when excess heating occurs the reactor core (like any material) will expand, becoming less dense. As it becomes less dense, neutrons will escape more easily into the structural material, and so will be removed from the chain-reaction cycle.

In addition, the reactor must be safeguarded against any accident that could cause any loss of the water in the core. For example, in case one of the pipes that carry this water ruptures, there must be some mechanism for replacing water in the core of the reactor. In general, these methods are referred to as the emergency core-cooling system. In a typical pressurized-water reactor, there are three systems, which should be independently operable. The main system, known as the accumulator, consists of water under high pressure. When the pressure of the water circulating in the core drops because of a break in one of the pipes, water from the accumulator is automatically injected into the reactor vessel. There is also a second emergency system of water under high pressure—water that can be injected into the primary water system in case of a slow depressurization or a small leak. And there is a low-pressure water-injection system, which is designed to replace the usual cooling loop once the temperature of the core has been reduced. This third system is designed to operate for as long as ninety days. For many years, doubts were raised about the effectiveness of the emergency core-cooling system. In 1978 and 1979, however, two exacting tests of it were made at a test facility in Idaho. In those tests, the system performed just as had been expected—in fact, better, because the core became less hot than had been predicted. The Idaho test reactor is a scaled-down model of a real power reactor—about one-sixth the size—but the water-flow systems are an exact replica. Before the tests were carried out, computer calculations were made at Idaho and at Los Alamos to predict what would happen. In particular, the precise time at which the water flow would be restored to the reactor was predicted, and the prediction was confirmed. This gives one considerable confidence that in an emergency the core-cooling system will work as it should. At Three Mile Island, the difficulties were not in the operation of the system but in the actions of the human operators who interfered with it.

Indeed, when one looks at these arrangements in the planning diagrams in, say, a typical nuclear-engineering text, it appears that the reactor designers have thought of everything that could go wrong. Yet obviously no one could have predicted the exact sequence of events that led to either of the two most serious accidents that have occurred in nuclear power plants—the Three Mile Island accident, and the accident at Browns Ferry, which preceded it by four years. The Browns Ferry Nuclear Power Plant, which is on the Tennessee River near Decatur, Alabama, is one of the largest electricity-generating facilities in the world. At present, it consists of three reactors that, combined, generate six percent of the electricity produced by nuclear power in the United States. The Tennessee Valley Authority began building it in 1966, and on August 1, 1974, it went into commercial operation with one reactor. A second reactor began operating early the following March, and the third in March of 1977. Shortly after noon on March 22, 1975, an electrician, Larry Hargett, was testing for air leaks in the cable room—a room beneath the plant's control room, which adjoined the containment buildings housing the reactors and their steam generators. The air pressure in a containment building is kept at less than normal atmospheric pressure, so that if a malfunction causes the fuel rods to leak radioactive material, this material will not spread outside the containment facility. There are holes in a containment building through which pipes and electrical cables pass in to the reactor and the steam generators. There had been a recent modification in the cable room, and a hole through which cables ran had just been stuffed by Hargett and an associate with strips of polyurethane foam, which is flammable. After stuffing the hole, Hargett wanted to see if he had made it airtight, and he used what was then the standard procedure to test for leaks—a lighted candle, whose flame would be drawn by any leak into the low-pressure containment building. When he held his candle close to the hole, he found that it had not been completely sealed, for the flame was sucked horizontally into the hole. Then the insulation on the electrical cables caught fire. Hargett and his associate tried to douse the fire with fire extinguishers, but after about fifteen minutes they realized that they could not bring it under control, and they reported the fire to a guard. When firemen arrived, the plant operators instructed them not to use water on the spreading fire, because electrical equipment was involved; instead, they tried various types of chemical extinguishers. The fire burned out of control for seven and a half hours and damaged sixteen hundred electrical cables, of which six hundred and eighteen were related to the plant's safety systems.

Meanwhile, engineers in the control room were engaged in a desperate struggle to keep the reactors under control and then cool them down as the control room itself began filling up with smoke. It took about sixteen hours after the fire had started to bring both reactors to a normal shutdown. The engineers accomplished this by bringing into play one of three auxiliary water supplies, which, while not part of the original emergency safety plan for the reactors, were adapted to that use. In the end, the fire caused many millions of dollars' worth of damage, and the power facility was restored only after eighteen months. Still, there were no serious injuries; there was no meltdown of the cores; and there was no release of radioactivity.

Clearly, no one ever wants a repetition of the Browns Ferry accident. But, just as clearly, it was as instructive an accident in terms of reactor safety as one could imagine. The material now used for cable insulation is unquestionably nonflammable, and it is a rule that all power reactors must have two different systems to supply electricity to the reactor safety equipment. And no one will ever again use an open flame to test for air leaks in a reactor plant.

The Browns Ferry accident is an illustration of the ability of human operators to prevent what might have been an extremely serious, possibly catastrophic incident. The Three Mile Island accident appears to be an illustration of nearly the opposite. If human operators had not intervened, this grave incident would probably have been a relatively minor one. In the normal operation of a pressurized-water power reactor, the primary cooling water flows into the reactor core through stainless steel pipes. The same water is pumped continuously through the system, absorbing heat in the reactor and giving it up again in the steam generators. This water becomes slightly radioactive, because the neutrons passing through it will react with the oxygen or any possible impurities in the water. The water in the secondary loops—which enters the generators, turns to steam to drive the electric turbines, and condenses—does not come in contact with either the reactor core or the radioactive water. The two systems flow alongside each other in the steam generators, and the cooler secondary water absorbs the heat of the primary water, which is transferred through the pipes. No radioactive water is turned to steam. To maintain the required degree of coolness in the reactor core, the secondary loops must constantly draw the heat away; otherwise, the primary water would get constantly hotter and would eventually evaporate, leaving the core exposed.

At 4 A.M. on Wednesday, March 28th, 1979, a series of pumps that were circulating water in the main-feed water system at Unit 2 of the Three Mile Island nuclear power station—one of the plant's two reactor units—tripped. This meant that the main mechanism for removing heat from the reactor was interrupted. The unit's two steam generators dried out and the primary water rapidly heated up. After about two minutes, both steam generators were completely dry. Before this happened they were supposed to have been supplied with water by emergency backup systems: three pumps, two electric and one steam-driven—but the discharge lines from these pumps were closed, a fact that was not discovered until eight minutes into the accident. Two block valves that should have been open at all times had been closed sometime before the accident. Meanwhile, the increasing temperature of the primary water had caused the pressure in that system to build up. Actually, the buildup had taken place in a few seconds, and a relief valve in a pressurizer tank had opened automatically, reducing the pressure in the primary water system to its normal level by releasing some of the radioactive water into a drain tank on the floor of the containment building. The valve leaked. (This, in fact, was known prior to the accident, and the leaky valve was supposed to have been replaced.) Consequently, water—mostly in the form of steam—was continuing to flow out through it, and the pressure within the system was continuing to drop. The drop in pressure automatically activated the emergency core-cooling system, which began pumping water into the primary system to replace the water being lost. It was at that point that the reactor operators made a serious error. They shut off the emergency water. Their reason for doing so seems to have been a misinterpretation of various confusing signals from the reactor. There was an indicator that showed the water level rising in the pressurizer tank. The operators assumed that the rise in the water level meant that the emergency water had overfilled the primary system and thus that the core was safely under water. In reality, the relief valve was still open, and the water from the emergency core-cooling system was escaping through it. When the system was turned off, the water pressure dropped again. After five and a half minutes, what was circulating in the primary system was a mixture of water and steam, and the core was on the way to becoming uncovered.

The water that escaped through the relief valve overflowed the drain tank on the floor of the containment building. The core became so hot that the fuel rods cracked and fission fragments escaped, and so this water contained considerably more radioactivity than normal. The radioactive overflow was pumped into tanks in an auxiliary building which were not designed to hold high pressures, and some of the radioactive steam from this water was released into the atmosphere through the building's ventilation system. Most of the radioactivity that escaped from the Three Mile Island reactor did so in this fashion. At 6:22 A.M., the operators, having finally realized that the relief valve on the pressurizer tank might be stuck open, closed a backup valve to seal the primary coolant system.

5 / The Problem

At 7:45 A.M., the Nuclear Regulatory Commission was notified that something was wrong at Three Mile Island. By about 9 A.M., the President had been informed, and the first news of the incident had reached the public.

In the meantime, a chemical reaction was taking place within the reactor. The top part of the reactor core, which was no longer covered with water, reached a temperature perhaps as high as four thousand degrees Fahrenheit, and the zirconium in which the fuel rods were encased reacted with water to produce zirconium oxide and free hydrogen. The hydrogen began to accumulate as a bubble at the top of the reactor vessel. On Friday afternoon, the Nuclear Regulatory Commission dispatched a dozen technical experts to Three Mile Island, and these people realized that, for two reasons, the expanding hydrogen bubble was a potential cause of alarm. In the first place, the bubble, as it expanded, could force down the level of the water cooling the core, and thus expose the core to even more extreme temperatures. (Even though the chain reaction in the reactor had been stopped by the control rods almost at once, the fission products continued to generate heat.) In the second place, hydrogen and oxygen are an explosive mixture when the oxygen reaches a certain concentration. (Hydrogen and oxygen, in combining to form water molecules, release a great deal of energy.) It was assumed—wrongly—that because oxygen might be accumulating from the breakup of water molecules, such a mixture might be building up in the reactor vessel, and there was concern that it might explode and possibly rip open the containment building, with a huge release of radioactivity. On Friday evening, Harold Denton, director of the N.R.C.'s Office of Nuclear Reactor Regulation, briefed Richard Thornburgh, the governor of Pennsylvania, about the gas bubble. Governor Thornburgh had already issued an advisory that pregnant women and young children keep more than five miles away from the plant. It was recognized that in the atmosphere of crisis so many conflicting theories had been generated that making coherent plans was all but impossible. Indeed, the chairman of the Nuclear Regulatory Commission, Joseph M. Hendrie, said at the time that he and the Governor were being forced to operate "almost totally in the blind," and added, "His information is ambiguous, mine is nonexistent, and—I don't know, it's like a couple of blind men staggering around making decisions." In retrospect, it is clear that there was never any real danger of a chemical explosion—and this is something that the Nuclear Regulatory Commission must have realized by the following Sunday, at the latest. Oxygen could have been produced, in principle, by the decomposition of the water by radiation. But there was, in fact, never any significant amount of oxygen produced. This fact was never explained to the public, and until the next week, at least, the general feeling was that we were all living on the edge of catastrophe. Only on Tuesday, April 10th, in testimony before a congressional subcommittee, did Hendrie state that an explosion could not have taken place, since "little, if any, oxygen" was present in the bubble.

Before discussing the implications of this accident for the future of nuclear power, I asked Bethe what the worst possible case at Three Mile Island might have been.

"People are always fascinated by the worst possible case, without clearly understanding that these worst cases are wildly improbable," Bethe said. "This emphasis on the worst possible case can do positive harm. In fact, the President's Commission investigating the Three Mile Island accident pointed out forcibly that the Nuclear Regulatory

Commission has devoted far too much effort to examining major potential accidents such as large breaks in pipes carrying the coolant, and that it should, rather, have instructed the utilities how to prevent and deal with lesser accidents, such as the series of mishaps that led to the situation at Three Mile Island. The member of the President's Commission living closest to Three Mile Island, Anne D. Trunk, noted in a supplemental view to the commission's report that during the accident the news coverage—especially the evening national-news reports by the major networks—emphasized too much the 'what if' rather than the 'what is,' and said, 'As a result, the public was pulled into a state of terror, of psychological stress.' Three Mile Island did not generate a meltdown, although the full extent of the damage to the core is not yet known. Even a meltdown, however, would not necessarily mean a major hazard to the public. Let us suppose that in a future accident, in spite of all safety devices, a meltdown actually takes place. Then the fission products that are normally contained within the fuel rods can escape, and can move around freely inside the reactor vessel. It will take somewhere between a half hour and an hour for the molten fuel to melt the steel wall of the reactor vessel itself. During this time, many of the fission products decay. There is much less radioactivity at the end of that time than there was at the beginning. So this time lapse is very important.

"Once the steel has melted, the fission products—a molten pool—would spread over the floor of the containment building. Inside the containment building, there are auxiliary safety systems. In particular, there is a spray system that is designed to cool the atmosphere in the building. Activating the spray system, which is done automatically at a much earlier stage of the accident, will reduce the pressure in the building, and at the same time it will condense some of the fission products that have been released as gases. Fission products run throughout the periodic table, and some of them can be condensed by cooling the atmosphere and some cannot. Xenon and krypton cannot be condensed, but if they are released into the atmosphere they are relatively harmless, because they just pass over as a cloud, and don't make fallout. Iodine does not condense easily at high temperatures, but if it is released into the colder outside air it can produce fallout, and this would constitute the main hazard, although this, too, is mitigated by using an iodine absorbing material in the spray system. Most of the strontium would be condensed within the containment building, and as for the plutonium, only a minute fraction of it will evaporate in the first place. The radioactive gases that do not condense are confined within the containment building. In fact, because the containment building is designed to withstand very high pressures, in the vast majority of these hypothetical accidents the radioactivity will be confined within the containment building itself. There is, of course, the China syndrome—that is, the molten fuel melting the floor of the reactor building and passing into the earth underneath. But there it will be well confined, and will not get into the atmosphere. A difficult but feasible mining operation could probably remove it.

"Danger to the public comes only when, after a meltdown, a break occurs in the containment building. It is clear that many unfortunate events have to occur in succession before this happens, and so it must be a rare event. If it ever does happen, then the radioactive materials that are still gases will be released into the atmosphere. Even then, however, the effects on the public will not really be as catastrophic as they are pictured in many popular accounts. It is just impossible that an area the size of Pennsylvania—some forty-five thousand square miles—will be made uninhabitable. In a really bad accident, the area that might become unusable is on the order of twenty to two hundred square miles. Perhaps an area ten times as large will have to be decontaminated by removing radioactive cesium and strontium from houses, streets, and so on. It has been predicted that unless the accident occurs at a time of unusually bad weather, no member of the public will die of radiation sickness within weeks. However, the radioactive fallout may cause delayed cancers. In estimating the number of such cancers that may be expected, one commonly uses the method put forth in the early seventies by the Committee on Biological Effects of Ionizing Radiation of the National Academy of Sciences—the so-called linear hypothesis, according to which a given amount of radiation causes the same number of cancers whether it is distributed over a thousand or a million people. With this hypothesis, it has been estimated that the delayed cancers caused by a bad accident in average weather conditions may be about a thousand in the course of thirty years. More recent detailed biological evidence indicates that small doses of gamma rays are considerably less dangerous in causing cancers than the linear hypothesis predicts, so the estimate is probably too high. In any case, since in the population affected by the fallout there will develop over the same thirty years about three hundred thousand cancers from other causes, it will be nearly impossible to tell whether the fallout has increased the cancer incidence, even statistically.

"But much more important than speculating on the worst possible case is to see what we can learn from the Three Mile Island accident. One of my friends said, 'After this ac-

cident, reactors will be much safer than they were before.'
He is right. Regrettable as Three Mile Island was, it has
taught us a lot about how to improve reactor safety. Probably the most important change will be to display much
clearer signals to the operators concerning the condition
of the reactor. For instance, it would be easy to have a
signal indicating that the water cooling the reactor will
begin to boil unless the pressure is increased—which can be
done through the emergency core-cooling system. There
should also be a signal indicating that the relief valve on
the pressurizer tank is open when it should be closed. At
present, it seems, the operators get too many signals, so
the important ones do not stand out. Edward Teller has
suggested going further. Many data are constantly measured in the reactor, but it is difficult for an operator to
put them together and draw the right conclusion quickly
enough, so Teller suggests that this be done by a computer. The operator could ask the computer 'What is going
to happen if I turn Valve No. 13?' and the computer would
give the answer. The judgment would be left to the operator, but the time-consuming analysis of the state of the
reactor would be done by the computer.

"The sequence of events that led to the Three Mile Island accident was listed as one of about seventy sequences
in the 1975 Rasmussen report on reactor safety. That list
should be used in the training of all operators; they should
be trained to respond quickly to any sequence. Since Three
Mile Island, better instructions have already been given to
operators. Generally, not only should the training of operators be improved but it should be recognized that operators have a great responsibility, similar to that of air-
plane pilots. The dignity of the profession should be raised,
and the pay made commensurate with the responsibility.

Technical help was apparently made available to Three Mile Island quickly, but the provision of such help could be planned ahead of time. An important requirement is to have the best technical competence available in the Nuclear Regulatory Commission."

Bethe made this analysis in the summer of 1979; this was before the President's Commission on the Accident at Three Mile Island, headed by John G. Kemeny, the president of Dartmouth, issued its report in the fall. The technical analysis of the accident given in the report is essentially the same as Bethe's. The commission emphasized the need for better training of reactor operators as well as for improvement in the way signals are displayed on the control panels. Concerning the severity of the accident itself, the report notes:

> Based on our investigation of the health effects of the accident, we conclude that in spite of serious damage to the plant, most of the radiation was contained and the actual release will have a negligible effect on the physical health of individuals. The major health effect of the accident was found to be mental stress.

It then goes on:

> Our calculations show that even if a meltdown occurred, there is a high probability that the containment building and the hard rock on which the TMI-2 containment building is built would have been able to prevent the escape of a large amount of radioactivity. These results derive from very careful calculations, which hold only insofar as our assumptions are valid. We cannot be absolutely certain of these results.

The commission was also highly critical of the N.R.C., especially of its licensing procedures and of its approach to reactor safety. It called for a complete revision of the N.R.C.'s procedures and attitudes, and even of its basic structure. The report emphasized that the licensing of nuclear reactors should be contingent on "the competency of the prospective operating licensee to manage the plant and the adequacy of its training program for operating personnel." In addition, licensing should be contingent upon "review and approval of the state and local emergency plans." As the commission emphasized, if nuclear power is to have a future in this country it must become clear to the public that the Three Mile Island accident has provoked a real change—and not a cosmetic one—in attitude toward nuclear safety on the part of all concerned.

When I discussed the Kemeny report with Bethe, he said that he agreed with its recommendations. He added that it was essential to have procedures that would guarantee that the people making decisions in the event of an accident had accurate information—which was not the case at Three Mile Island. An accident does not necessarily constitute an emergency, and even in an emergency the response, in the words of the Kemeny report, "may range from evacuation of an area near the plant, to the distribution of potassium iodide to protect the thyroid gland from radioactive iodine, to a simple instruction to people several miles from the plant to stay indoors for a specified period of time."

What effect has the Three Mile Island accident had on the nuclear power programs of other countries? So far, it appears to have had very little. France and the Soviet Union are continuing the development of nuclear power as rapidly as possible. The Russians, however, according to recent reports, are now building, for the first time—as a response to Three Mile Island—concrete containment buildings around their reactors. The French have little choice if they are to maintain their present standard of living, for France has essentially nothing in the way of alternative energy sources. Still, like the Soviet Union, it does have a large pool of technological skills to draw on. Whatever other lessons Three Mile Island teaches, it has shown that having such technology available is an absolute necessity in any emergency situation. Though the local power company that operated the Three Mile Island plant—Metropolitan Edison—simply did not have the personnel to deal with the crisis it found itself in, people who could deal with it were available elsewhere in the country, and could be brought in to help control a rapidly deteriorating and extremely dangerous situation.

But what about Third World countries? In a recently published article in *Nature*, Anil Agarwal concludes:

> From all present indications, it seems that the incident of Three Mile Island has scarcely sent a ripple through those Third World countries which are keen to buy and build as many nuclear reactors as they can. Part of the reason for this behavior is that nuclear programs have come to be associated by developing countries with enormous political prestige. The efforts of Western governments to control the spread of nuclear technologies are seen by many Third World governments as a crude attempt to monopolize a technology that is of considerable importance to the world. These discriminatory Western pressures have helped to make nuclear power, as a senior IAEA [International Atomic Energy Agency] official recently put it, "an immensely patriotic issue" in many developing countries and even in some developed ones like Japan. Under these circumstances, nuclear authorities in Third World countries will move very cautiously to accept safety-related arguments against nuclear power.

In a recent referendum, the Swedish people, who have one of the highest per capita energy consumption rates in the world and very large deposits of uranium, voted to continue their program of nuclear power even though the present Swedish government is opposed to it.

Beyond the matter of national prestige, there is enormous economic pressure in these countries to keep power reactors running, even when they do not meet proper safety standards. The closing of a reactor could mean the loss of a significant percentage of the country's electric power. Agarwal gives an example. Much of the electric power for the city of Bombay is supplied by the Tarapur Atomic Power Station, known as TAPS. It was built in 1969 by General Electric, and was the first nuclear power station to go into operation in the Third World. It now appears that it has for some time been using defective fuel bundles, with the result that the amount of radioactivity in the plant during normal operation is well above acceptable safety levels. Agarwal quotes from the journal *Business India:* "TAPS is so heavily contaminated . . . that it is impossible for maintenance jobs to be performed without the maintenance personnel exceeding the fortnightly dose of 400 millirem in a matter of minutes. Thus the maintenance worker—who is often not an employee of TAPS—holding a spanner in one hand and a pencil dosimeter in the other, turning a nut two, three rotations and rushing out of the work area is a common phenomenon in TAPS." When a TAPS engineer was asked why the plant was not shut down for decontamination, he replied, Agarwal says, "Ideally, that should have been done in 1974 or earlier, but there is such great pressure from the Department of Atomic Energy on us to produce power that we cannot shut down." Even so, India at least has a large pool of trained nuclear engineers, whereas many of the other Third World countries have neither trained personnel nor a body that, like the Nuclear Regulatory Commission, has the authority to oversee the safety of nuclear plants. The I.A.E.A. is planning to organize an emergency-assistance program to fly experts from one country to another in case of an accident. But the accidents at Browns Ferry and Three Mile Island illustrate how vital it is to be able to take effective action in a matter of minutes. What is needed if Third World plants are going to be kept running at an acceptable level of safety is internationally recognized standards, and also clearly defined and accepted guidelines for the number of operators and the level of their training. Similar international standards seem to be accepted by the aviation industry, and surely they are as urgently needed in the nuclear power industry.

Without a supply of uranium that is guaranteed to last for some time, no utility company will invest in a billion-dollar plant designed to use that fuel. A nuclear research engineer for one of the largest Midwestern utility companies said to me recently, "No utility company wants to be in the position of having ordered the *last* of the nuclear power stations. It would be like buying the last gasoline-burning automobile." For this reason—and because of safety and economics—orders for new nuclear-plant construction have come to almost a dead stop in this country, the construction workers who build the plants are being laid off, and the number of students going into nuclear engineering is decreasing.

In addition to apprehensions about the safety and the environmental impact of nuclear power, there is deep concern over the possibility that the proliferation of nuclear reactors will lead to a proliferation of nuclear weapons—some of which, it is feared, may fall into the hands of irresponsible governments or of terrorist groups. This fear certainly appears to be a significant factor in the policies of the Carter Administration toward nuclear energy—policies that, intentionally or not, may bring our development of nuclear power to an end. The heart of the matter is whether and in what way the development of large numbers of nuclear power stations can increase the availability of plutonium and whether this plutonium can be obtained by governments or individuals who should not have it. As we have seen, nuclear fuel does not initially contain plutonium but consists of a nonexplosive mixture of U-235 and U-238; plutonium does not occur naturally but is made in a reactor. For making a bomb, the necessary isotope of plutonium is Pu-239. In a power reactor, Pu-239 is produced in three stages. First, a neutron is captured by a U-238 nucleus to produce U-239. This is an unstable isotope, and it decays, by the emission of an electron, into an isotope of neptunium, Np-239, which, in turn, decays by electron emission into Pu-239. Another isotope of plutonium, Pu-240, is also produced. Pu-240 is not suitable for making a bomb, because it emits neutrons spontaneously and copiously, and these may ignite the bomb material prematurely and produce a greatly reduced explosion —a fizzle. The plutonium that is produced in a power reactor is therefore not ideal for making nuclear weapons. Indeed, when India made its nuclear device, what the scientists used for making plutonium was not a power reactor but a specially designed research reactor, which made sizable quantities of Pu-239 and very little Pu-240.

Nonetheless, in a year a power reactor produces about a hundred and thirty kilograms of Pu-239, which remains in the fuel rods. The "reprocessing" of nuclear waste involves the separation of this isotope of plutonium from the fission fragments and the uranium also remaining in the rods. When the rods are removed from a working reactor, they still contain about a third as much fissionable material as they did when they went into the reactor. Since this is valuable, no power company simply wants to throw it away by burying it in a hole two thousand feet deep. In any event, no such hole currently exists, so—temporarily, at least—the rods are sitting at the bottom of the specially designed pools of water. Anyone who tried to steal either the stored rods or the rods in a working reactor would be mad—suicidal. The rods are so hot, in both their actual temperature and their radioactivity, that to steal one would mean certain and rapid death. (The water cools the rods to about one hundred and twenty degrees Fahrenheit. In air they would be over seven hundred degrees.)

The serious problem would be the availability of plutonium if the partly spent fuel elements are reprocessed. The idea is to split the fuel elements by chemical means. The fission fragments are separated from the uranium and plutonium, and these two elements are then separated from each other. The fission fragments are considered waste, and are safely disposed of accordingly. The uranium may be returned to an isotope-separation plant to be reenriched, or it may be used in making new fuel elements. The plutonium could be either added to the fuel for the present generation of reactors or saved for future use in breeders. The concern is that if this scheme were followed, the plutonium might be stolen and used for the illicit manufacture of atomic bombs, and very careful measures would have to be taken to prevent such thefts. This is, in Bethe's view, a valid reason for the Carter Administration to have been adamant about not selling reprocessing plants abroad. But in addition, in 1976, President Ford stopped the develop-

ment and operation of chemical reprocessing plants here—
a measure that President Carter has strongly reaffirmed.
In this way, the President hopes to set a moral example for
the other nuclear nations. In the main, however, this has
not been very successful. It has had some benefit in that
it has discouraged at least temporarily, the Germans and
the French from selling reprocessing plants abroad. But
many of the nuclear countries (including the Soviet Union) are either reprocessing now or tooling up to do it.
Their uranium economy just will not function otherwise.
So these countries are not making the slightest effort to
follow our "example," and probably consider it merely
confirmation of their notion that our energy policy borders
on the irrational.

If our nuclear-fission program were in fact now coming to
an end, what would that mean? This is a question that I
explored in detail with Bethe. One can suppose, for argument's sake, that our energy consumption will remain fixed
at its present level. If one allows for growth, the numbers
will look a lot worse; if one assumes that we will conserve
radically, the numbers will look somewhat better. But suppose that we want to live exactly as we do today—to use
the same number of kilowatt-hours from year to year.
Physicists distinguish between two types of kilowatts—
thermal kilowatts, which indicate the rate at which fuel
energy is released by burning; and electrical kilowatts,
which are what we use when we turn on a light switch.
In burning fuel to make electricity, there is an inevitable
loss of energy, owing to the Second Law of Thermodynamics. The Second Law puts a powerful constraint on the
efficiency with which thermal energy can be turned into
electrical energy. Though engineers have been working

hard to cut this loss to a minimum, it is unlikely that it can be reduced below a half. With the present machinery for going from thermal kilowatts to electrical kilowatts, there is a loss of about two-thirds; that is to say, one-third of the thermal energy is converted into electrical energy.

If we express all our energy sources in terms of the electricity that could be made from them, whether or not the energy is actually made into electricity or provided in other forms, the United States uses about seven and a half trillion kilowatt-hours electrical each year. (The Technical Glossary discusses the conversion of this unit into other commonly used units.) Of this energy, natural gas gives us two trillion two hundred billion kilowatt-hours. Domestic oil, foreign oil, and coal give about one and a half trillion kilowatt-hours each. An additional amount of about six hundred billion kilowatt-hours of electrical energy is supplied by hydro-electric and nuclear power. Hydroelectric power, which, as has been noted, we are already using to essentially the fullest extent possible, is highly efficient: nearly all the kinetic energy of the water can be converted into electricity. A nuclear power plant, as plants are now designed, has only about a thirty-three percent efficiency.

According to the best estimates, our known domestic supply of natural gas will be used up in about a decade. If the unproved reserves are as large as some estimates suggest, the supply might be prolonged until perhaps the year 2020. By that time, our known reserves of domestic oil will also have run out. This means that just to maintain our present total energy consumption we will have to find another source to produce more than three and a half trillion kilowatt-hours of energy each year. In the absence of nuclear energy, the only real alternative is coal. This means that in the year 2020 we will have to mine at least four times as much coal as we are mining now; in other words, we will have to mine some two and a half billion tons of coal a year. Most of the new coal will have to come from strip mining in the Western states; Eastern coal mines are, in general, old mines, and most of the coal that it is practical to mine in the East is being mined. This means that the coal will have to be shipped, on the average, something like a thousand miles to where it is to be used; that is, from Western mines to Eastern cities. The present total railroad use in the United States is about a trillion ton-miles a year. But if we have to rely on coal, our railroads will have to carry about two trillion four hundred billion ton-miles in the year 2020 just to ship coal; that is, even if we want to ship only coal, and nothing else, on the railroads, we must at least double their capacity in the next forty years. Yet at present our railroad system is in a state of decay. Moreover, the environmental impact of quadrupling coal production and burning so much coal must be considered, and so must the consequences of having our entire energy production in the hands of one industry—the coal industry. (It would also be possible to transport coal dust suspended in water-liquified coal. But then pipelines would have to be constructed. Some coal, about twenty percent, is now carried in trucks and on barges. There does not seem to be, however, any realistic possibility of expanding these alternate forms of transportation for Western coal.)

Even if we do manage to replace our depleted domestic oil and natural-gas supplies with coal, we will still be running short of energy raw material. We cannot assume that we will be able to continue to import foreign oil in the present quantities, since that oil is also running out. So a large part of this gap will also have to be filled with coal. It has frequently been suggested that we should fill some of the gap by using biomass—animal and human wastes and such agricultural waste as cornstalks. This material burns only about half as efficiently as coal. It is also widely dispersed, so its collection would require a great deal of transportation—which would require more energy. If all the biomass produced in the United States in one year were burned, it would be the equivalent of a billion tons of coal, or about half of our projected needs in forty years. This could make a dent in the energy problem, but the cost of transportation and of construction of the facilities needed to convert biomass into fuel has to be taken into account, as does the additional energy needed for the transportation, construction, and conversion.

Of course, some of the energy that must be replaced could come from nuclear sources. But unless there is a change in attitude toward nuclear energy in this country, that will soon cease to be an option. Since 1972, the American utilities industry has cancelled the construction of fifty-nine nuclear power stations, for reasons having to do with the present complicated licensing procedures, the failure of the federal government to provide a long-term waste-disposal site, which it was mandated to do by Congress in 1970, and the uncertainty of the uranium supplies, as well as with the public view of the safety and environmental problems presented by nuclear plants. Another important reason is that the growth in demand for electricity has slowed since 1973. In the very near future, our country must make a clear-cut decision about nuclear power. The present unsettled situation simply delays the decision to the point where events will decide things for us. The rest of the technologically developed world has already made its decision, and—on a governmental level, at least—has proceeded with nuclear technology, to the point where American technology has fallen behind. And this gap continues to widen.

In other industrialized countries, the research and development of nuclear technology are focused on the preservation and manufacture of nuclear fuel. In any such schemes, reprocessing of the fuel elements plays a crucial role. The United States may shortly be the only nuclear country that does not reprocess. (The British government has just approved the construction of the largest reprocessing facility in the world, at Windscale, in northwest England.) We are at present using uranium in our nuclear power program in about the most wasteful way imaginable.

Most of the nuclear power stations under construction here are gigawatt stations, one gigawatt being a million kilowatts. It would take about four hundred gigawatt stations to produce the electricity now being produced by fossil fuels, and using such stations would free the fossil fuels for things that other energy sources cannot be used for—transportation and petrochemicals among them.

But a gigawatt light-water reactor consumes about a ton of U-235 in a year. It returns about two hundred and fifty kilograms of plutonium. At any given time, it contains about ninety tons of U-238, which cannot be used as fuel in such reactors, because thermal neutrons will not fission U-238. In other words, these reactors extract about six-tenths of one percent of the potential energy content of the uranium. Yet we can extend our uranium supply by about forty percent even if we continue to use light-water reactors simply by reprocessing the partly spent fuel elements. Beyond that, we can make enormously impressive qualitative changes in the fuel situation by upgrading reactor technology. These are not futuristic ideas; prototype models are now in active use abroad.

Light water is not an especially good moderator. The reason is an interesting bit of nuclear physics. A water molecule consists of two protons and an oxygen nucleus, along with a cloud of electrons that don't play any role in the nuclear physics, since they are far away from the nucleus. When a fast neutron is produced in a fission, it escapes from the fuel element and enters the moderator—in this case, water. It now begins to collide with the protons and the oxygen nuclei in the water molecules. Some of the collisions are elastic; that is, the neutron simply bounces off one of these particles. After about twenty such collisions, the neutron is slowed down enough—has lost enough energy—so that it can cause further fissions of the U-235 or the Pu-239. Elastic collisions are not the only thing that can happen to the neutron, however. It can be absorbed by the water. Or it can be captured by the uranium without fission—another source of neutron loss. A neutron and a proton can collide and combine to form a nucleus of heavy hydrogen—a deuteron, which consists of one neutron and one proton. When that happens, the fission neutron is removed from the fuel cycle. It turns out that the neutron capture by protons is a fairly likely process. This is the reason a light-water reactor will work only with fuel that has been enriched with U-235 or Pu-239; in a light-water reactor using natural uranium, too many neutrons are absorbed by the moderator and by the U-238.

If instead of using ordinary water as the moderator, however, one uses heavy water, the situation changes. The molecule of heavy water consists of two deuterons and an oxygen nucleus, and neutron capture by a deuteron is only about five ten-thousandths as likely as capture by the proton alone, the reason being the neutron in the deuteron nucleus. Since an oxygen nucleus captures very few neutrons, heavy water is such a good moderator that heavy-water reactors can be fuelled by natural uranium, with no enriching admixture of U-235. This is a great economy factor, because isotope separation is a difficult and costly business. Heavy-water power reactors are now in use in Ontario and Quebec, and these, which are known as CANDU (Canadian Deuterium Uranium) reactors, have been exported to Pakistan, India, Korea, and Argentina. Bethe regards the CANDU as a "technical wonder," and told me, "Not only is it very conservative in fuel but it works with a regularity and reliability that are absolutely fantastic. The reactor seems to be practically always available. Our reactors, because of the need to replace spent fuel rods and to do other maintenance work, are available only seventy to eighty percent of the time, but the CANDU, because it can refuel without shutting down, is available ninety percent of the time." The drawback is the price. It is expensive to separate heavy water from ordinary water, and, besides, additional plumbing must be designed to insure that none of the water gets lost in the working cycle of the reactor. This and other design features add about twenty-five percent to the cost of building such a power station, but the countries that have invested in reactors of the CANDU type have decided that this extra cost is compensated for by the economies that such a reactor makes possible.

With the help of reprocessing and the use of slightly enriched fuel, Bethe pointed out to me, the CANDU would be able to do so well in preserving nuclear fuel that it would look at first sight as if it did not use up any fuel at all. To understand this, one must trace the route of the fission neutrons in this type of reactor. When the U-235 fissions, something over two neutrons—on the average—are released. One of these neutrons goes on to make the next fission, which sustains the chain reaction. In a light-water reactor, the other neutron tends to get absorbed by the structure of the reactor itself, by the fission fragments, or, most frequently, by the water moderator. In the heavy-water reactor, this last source of absorption is essentially eliminated, so the extra neutrons reenter the uranium fuel —mostly U-238—often enough to cause a conversion of a U-238 nucleus into plutonium, which is as good as the original U-235 for the chain reaction. Thus, ideally, in a heavy-water reactor there is for each U-235 nucleus split a Pu-239 nucleus created, and no loss of fuel. However, neutrons do still get absorbed by fission fragments and the reactor structure, so the conversion is not complete. To increase the efficiency even of a heavy-water reactor, fission fragments must be separated from the uranium every two or three years—and that once again raises the issue of reprocessing. A reactor with similar performance characteristics is being developed in this country by the Naval Branch of the Reactor Division of the Department of Energy. It has been built in Shippingport, near Pittsburgh, and is reported to be a near breeder like the CANDU. It is, unlike the CANDU, a light-water reactor, and therefore uses enriched uranium.

Bethe told me that an even better arrangement for a CANDU type of reactor would be to use U-235 mixed with thorium—an element more plentiful than uranium. If thorium is used, the extra neutrons will convert the thorium not into plutonium but into U-233, a lighter isotope of uranium, which is extremely rare in concentrations of natural uranium. As a fissionable material, U-233 is more efficient than either plutonium or U-235, and by using it one could reproduce, with reprocessing, well over ninety percent of the fissionable material that was originally put into such a reactor. One would have to supply only the remainder.

There is a reactor now being developed abroad that produces more fuel than it consumes. This is the so-called breeder. The notion of making a reactor that produces more fuel than it consumes goes back to the beginning of reactor technology. Bethe recalled a lecture that Fermi gave at Los Alamos just after the Second World War in which he said, perhaps overoptimistically, that the country that learned to build a breeder reactor would have solved its energy problems forever. (Bethe himself began working on the breeder concept, with emphasis on its safety aspects, in the late nineteen-forties.) In fact, the first reactor ever to produce electricity was a breeder—a so-called fast breeder—designed by Fermi with the physicist Walter Zinn; it was built in Idaho by the Argonne National Laboratory, and went into operation in 1951. It is likely that similar fast breeders will serve as the prototypes for the next generation of power reactors. However, because the Carter Administration has indicated opposition to the development of breeder reactors the field has been taken over by other countries—most notably France and the Soviet Union.

The essential feature of these reactors is that the neutrons in them are moderated as little as possible. The neutrons from a given fission remain "fast." Since fast neutrons fission even the common isotopes of uranium and thorium, these can now act in part as fuels. The main working fuel, however, is plutonium, which has particularly favorable properties when it is used with fast neutrons. In fact, breeder reactors, when they are developed, may provide an excellent way of "burning" excess plutonium and so reducing the amount of it available for potential use in nuclear weapons; the breeder can be made to consume rather than produce plutonium. Today, however, in the Phénix reactor, which went into operation in Marcoule, France, in 1973, the fuel consists of about eighty percent U-238 and about twenty percent plutonium. Its mixed-fuel rods form the interior of the core, and there is also a blanket of uranium rods surrounding the core. The breeding is done in this uranium blanket. It comes about because when fast neutrons fission Pu-239 about three neutrons are released. If none of the three are absorbed elsewhere, one is available for the next fission to keep the chain reaction going, and the two others can convert U-238 nuclei into plutonium. Ideally, then, two plutonium nuclei are created for each one that is split. In practice, there is parasitic neutron absorption, but, even so, the breeder will produce more plutonium than it consumes. (There has also been research on so-called slow breeders, which would use slow neutrons to convert thorium into U-233, but this technology has not advanced to the prototype stage.) The entire core is immersed in a pool of liquefied sodium, which serves to cool it. Water is not used because it slows down the neutrons. One advantage of these reactors is that the sodium coolant is at atmospheric pressure within the reactor, and this arrangement eliminates some of the problems associated with those reactors whose coolants have to be kept under high pressure.

The Phénix is basically a prototype and does not really breed significant amounts of plutonium, but now France, in collaboration with West Germany, Italy, Belgium, the Netherlands, and Britain, is constructing a Super-Phénix, at Creys-Malville, about thirty miles east of Lyons, which is designed to produce over a gigawatt of power and which will breed. In such a breeder, about two hundred and fifty kilograms of excess plutonium will be produced in a year, and it appears to be this fact—not only the safety aspects of the reactor—that caused the Carter Administration's reluctance to develop a breeder. The basic argument in favor of the breeder is that any country with a breeder reactor has nuclear independence. Any country that relies on a light-water reactor and does not have its own supplies of enriched uranium is forced to call upon a supplier country when it runs out of fuel, so the supplier can exert some control over how the consumer country uses the plutonium it manufactures in its reactors. If the consumer country is diverting plutonium to make weapons, the supplier country can simply withhold new fuel supplies—as we recently withheld them from India for a time. To this extent, Bethe agrees with President Carter's policy of not exporting either breeders or reprocessing facilities to non-nuclear nations, but he strongly disagrees with the corollary that President Carter appears to have decided on; namely, that in order to set an example for the other nuclear nations we should not have a breeder, either. It is partly for this reason that the Administration has requested the cancellation of funds for our large breeder prototype on the Clinch River, in Tennessee. Bethe feels that we should develop and test a workable breeder—not necessarily of the Clinch River design—in case we want to use breeders someday, especially since, whatever we may do, the other nuclear nations are building breeders, for the simple reason that they recognize their resources of coal and oil and uranium to be limited.

The safety of sodium-cooled, fast-breeder reactors has been a subject of study for many years. The working fuel is maintained in "pins" only a few millimeters in diameter. If such a pin develops a leak this is readily detectable since the fission products normally contained in the pin get into the sodium coolant, in which case the leaking pin is simply replaced. Another concern is that a pin may swell and inhibit the flow of the sodium. Experiments have been performed in which a given fuel pin was deliberately made to obstruct the flow of sodium, with the resulting observation that the neighboring pins remain adequately cooled. This is one of the factors that make a meltdown of such a breeder extremely unlikely. Moreover, sodium is a material with high heat conductivity, allowing local hot spots to be rapidly cooled. And the uranium-plutonium mixture, used as fuel, loses its efficiency for fission by fast neutrons when it is heated, thus causing the fission process to shut itself off. The fuel itself therefore acts as a kind of thermostat. Nonetheless, one must still take into account what could happen if there were a meltdown. The worry has been that if this happened, and the sodium coolant was expelled from the reactor, the fuel might assemble in a compact mass which could become "critical" for fast neutrons and hence explode. A long series of experiments done by the Argonne National Laboratory at the Idaho Testing Station, however, has shown that the opposite happens. The fuel tends to be dispersed under such conditions.

While experiments like these have convinced the European countries that breeder reactors are safe enough to be deployed, the program in this country, for reasons previously mentioned, is in limbo. Countries that are developing the breeder are doing so because they have a long-term commitment to nuclear energy as a partial solution to their energy problem and, given this commitment, they need an assured supply of uranium. The breeder solves the problem of uranium supply. From a given amount of uranium about sixty times as much energy can be extracted in a fast breeder than in a light-water reactor. But this multiplies the available fuel by a much greater factor, since more abundant lower grade uranium ores then become commercially exploitable. To get some idea of the numbers involved: imagine using uranium fission and breeders to supply *all* our energy needs—then given the present rate of consumption there is enough uranium ore available to last us for at least ten thousand years. However, the energy problem really consists of two energy problems. The first is the supply of total energy, and the second is the supply of portable fuel for transportation. In the United States, as we have mentioned, about a quarter of our energy budget goes into transportation and nearly all of this involves the use of oil, which translates into about half of our total oil consumption. (The rest goes into petrochemicals and other petroleum products.) No one proposes using nuclear energy for ordinary transportation. Nuclear energy and coal are to be used as substitute raw materials for oil and gas wherever this is possible. We simply cannot afford to continue to use oil and gas where they can be replaced by other sources; nor can we afford to continue to use these products at the same rate we have been doing—even for transportation. There is now evidence that this is a lesson that the American people are beginning to take seriously. Gasoline consumption declined by eight percent in the last quarter of 1979, and fuel-inefficient automobiles are becoming less and less marketable. In fact, until our manufacturers can produce automobiles, in large quantities, with the same fuel efficency as the European and Japanese models they will continue to lose the market to foreign competitors.

But these transformations are painfully slow. In California and Massachusetts, for example, over eighty percent of electricity is still being generated by using oil and gas.

Thirty percent of all homes are heated by oil, and sixty percent by gas. Since natural gas supplies are more abundant than oil it makes sense to convert all heating processes from oil to gas. And our homes can, and should, be much better insulated than they are now. Bethe likes the idea of "house doctors" of the sort that are envisioned in a bill recently introduced by Senator Bill Bradley of New Jersey. These would be people who are experts in house insulation, who have no financial axe to grind, and who would examine American houses to improve their heat efficiency. If this were done, it has been estimated that half the heating cost could be eliminated for living units. Even if this factor were reduced only by a third it would be savings enough so that if all the units presently using oil were converted to gas, no more gas would be used than is being used now. This kind of improvement in energy efficiency is already practiced successfully in industry, which uses about forty percent of our total energy supply. In many companies energy consumption has been reduced by as much as twenty-five percent without reducing output.

But even with all of this, it is likely that our oil supply will still be deficient. Bethe is convinced that we must begin to develop synthetic fuels of both oil and gas. For many years the price per barrel of these synthetics has been a matter of speculation. It is important to begin pilot projects to find the most efficient methods for their production and real cost. Congress has now authorized twenty billion dollars for such a project, and a private consortium has begun to manufacture synthetic gas in the Midwest. If synthetic petroleum is produced in sufficient quantity it can put a ceiling on the oil prices that foreign producers can charge us. This would put an end to declarations, such as the one made by the Libyan delegate to OPEC in 1979, that "the industrial countries will pay any price for oil." We must also keep in mind that conservation can really be done only once. After the waste has been eliminated it has been eliminated. Conservation does not manufacture energy.

Coal, which does manufacture energy, carries with it the problem of pollution. There is, to begin with, particulate pollution, or coal dust, which can be reduced by electrostatic precipitation. A good reason for centralized power production is that effective measures to combat pollution, such as the precipitation of the particulates, are easier to implement and carry out in one big power station than in a myriad of small coal burners. The infamous London fogs were largely due to millions of small coal dust particles sent into the air by, literally, hundreds of thousands of private coal fires—with water vapor condensing around the coal dust. With the introduction of central heating, which displaced open coal fireplaces, the dense fogs were virtually eliminated. Next, and more complicated, is the problem posed by the sulfur content of the coal. Sulfur, when burned, becomes sulfur dioxide and, in the air, may be converted into sulfuric acid, which falls to the earth as acid rain. New technologies such as the so-called "scrubbers" or "fluid-bed combustion" can be used to keep this source of pollution under control.

However, there is one pollution problem that cannot be avoided and it concerns all fossil fuels. When such fuels are burned they produce carbon dioxide, CO_2. While this substance is not directly harmful to humans, it may have a very serious effect on the climate. A committee formed by the National Academy of Science has made a careful study; its conclusion is that a doubling of the CO_2 content in the atmosphere would raise the average temperature of the

5 / The Problem

earth's surface by two to four degrees centigrade. The reason for the temperature rise is that CO_2 absorbs the infrared radiation which the earth's surface reemits into space after the sun heats it. The CO_2 lets in the visible light from the sun without disturbance but does not let all the earth's radiation out, especially the very long or infra-red wave lengths—behaving in this respect like the glass roof of a greenhouse—and hence the warming. A doubling of the CO_2 in the atmosphere would have very serious consequences for the global climate. From 1958 to 1979, the CO_2 content of the atmosphere rose by about six percent. Increased use of fossil fuels is likely to increase this rate, but there are so many uncertainties in the matter of where the CO_2 goes that it is hard to predict when the doubling would occur. Possibly in a hundred years, or somewhat earlier or later.

The production of CO_2 from burning coal is worse than from burning oil, and oil is worse than gas. In coal nearly all the energy comes from the burning of carbon to make CO_2. Oil is essentially CH_2, and a substantial part of the energy comes from burning the hydrogen to make water, which is harmless. Natural gas is CH_4 which contains even more hydrogen than oil. Hence, natural gas produces less CO_2 than oil, which, in turn, produces less than coal. If coal is used to make synthetic fuel this is even worse for the CO_2 problem than the direct burning of coal, since some CO_2 is also produced in the process of making the synthetic. If wood is used as a fuel this does not add to the CO_2, since growing the tree has absorbed as much CO_2 as is produced when the wood is burned. But this is only true as long as one does not burn more than the new growth of trees. For this reason deforestation is very detrimental because it diminishes green plants which can absorb CO_2, and if this deforestation comes about by *burning* trees then the damage is doubled. Biomass, or the growing of plants for the specific purpose of burning them for their energy content, is neutral with respect to CO_2—it neither increases nor decreases it. The same is true for the direct use of sunlight to produce energy. Nuclear energy does not produce CO_2. But it does produce heat as a byproduct, and much of this heat is used in the enhanced evaporation of water. This water condenses again and returns to earth as rain; it does not accumulate as a gas which can warm the earth, and thus contribute to climatic changes. The moral to be drawn is that while CO_2 does not pose an immediate threat it is something that must be watched carefully, and it may place an upper limit on the amount of fossil fuels which can ultimately be burned.

The reactors now in use produce energy by nuclear fission. It is also possible to build a reactor that produces power by nuclear fusion, but a working prototype of a fusion power plant does not currently exist anywhere in the world. The nearest place to find one is the sun. Indeed, the whole idea of fusion is to reproduce some of the characteristics of the sun's interior. The controlled-fusion research enterprise is nearly thirty years old, and at present the mood of the scientists engaged in it is generally hopeful. Bethe, for one, thinks that some form of crude power-producing fusion reactor may be realized in the mid-nineteen-eighties, and that in the next century fusion may be one of the common ways of achieving power production.

The interior temperature of the sun is estimated to be fourteen million degrees centigrade. Matter at such temperatures is in the form of a plasma gas that consists of free nuclei—mostly protons and helium—and the electrons that have been stripped from the corresponding atoms. This gas would simply fly apart under its own pressure if it were not that there is so much of it that the gravitational forces keep the sun's mass in equilibrium against this pressure. If any significant number of fusions are to be produced on earth, there must be a plasma kept at a working temperature of many millions of degrees, and some force must keep the plasma from flying apart. The reason for the high temperatures is that the collisions among the positively charged nuclei have to be violent enough to overcome the tendency of two like charges to repel each other—something that we discussed in connection with energy production in stars. In a laboratory, the latter objective is achieved by the use of high magnetic fields. A charged particle in a magnetic field will tend to move along the lines of that field, executing spirals around them. In fusion research, therefore, a magnetic field is designed in such a way as to confine the plasma within a limited space. Such a magnetic-field configuration is often referred to as a magnetic bottle. At each end of the bottle, the field lines converge, so that, ideally, a charged particle will spiral to the end and reverse itself, and continue to spiral back and forth indefinitely. In reality, the plasma, for various reasons, tends to develop instabilities, and these instabilities cause kinks—sharp bends—in the field lines, which make the bottle leak. For years, workers in the field of plasma physics were plagued by discoveries of new and unexpected ways in which instabilities developed, and it began to look as if no practical way would ever be found to confine a plasma magnetically. In the mid-nineteen-sixties, however, a group of Russian physicists hit upon a design that they called a TOKAMAK—an acronym for the Russian words meaning "toroidal magnetic chamber." It appears to offer great promise. In the area of magnetic-field confinement, most of the present fusion research, both here and abroad, is done on TOKA-MAKS, and several experimental models have been built.

The TOKAMAK looks like a large, fat metal doughnut—a torus—made of stainless steel. One of the largest such reactors in the world is now under construction at the Princeton Plasma Physics Laboratory. The outer circumference of the torus is seventy-five feet; the doughnut itself is six feet thick. A high vacuum is maintained inside a TOKA-MAK. Electrical wire is wrapped around the outside, and this produces magnetic fields to guide the charged plasma particles introduced into the vessel. Some of the wire is wrapped the long way around the doughnut, and some is wrapped in loops around the short way. By adjusting the strength of the magnetic fields produced by these separate windings, one can force a charged particle to move in orbits inside the torus. Experimental results showing that there is a reasonably stable confinement of the plasma in such machines have led to the present optimism over the future of the program. Moreover, the "confinement times" have increased from only 10^{-5} seconds in the magnetic bottles designed in 1955 to as much as a tenth of a second in the modern TOKAMAKS.

To make a TOKAMAK like the one being built at Princeton produce power, a mixture of deuterium and tritium will be injected into the vacuum vessel. (Tritium is another isotope of hydrogen—one whose mass is three times that of ordinary hydrogen.) This mixture will be heated to a temperature of a hundred million degrees Celsius—a process that, of course, consumes a great deal of energy. But as the mixture is heated and the electrons are stripped off by collisions, the nuclei—confined by the magnetic fields to a region where they encounter one another, and not the walls of the torus

—themselves will begin to collide. Energy is produced when a deuteron (consisting of a proton and a neutron) and a triton (consisting of two neutrons and a proton) collide, and fuse into a helium nucleus (consisting of two protons and two neutrons), with the release of an energetic neutron. (This reaction releases seventeen and a half million electron volts of energy, most of which is taken off by the released neutron. A fission reaction releases about two hundred million electron volts of energy, so fission is a much more energy-productive process.) In a future TOKAMAK power reactor, the vacuum vessel containing the plasma will be surrounded by a blanket of materials that absorb the neutrons, which emerge from the plasma at high speed. The kinetic energy of the neutrons will heat the blanket; the blanket is to be provided with pipes containing a cooling fluid to carry the heat away; and this heat will generate the steam to produce electricity.

One thing that is surprising about these machines is how little matter there actually is in the working plasma—the heated gas. Typically, there are about 10^{14} particles per cubic centimetre of the plasma, whereas in a solid the density is a billion times as great. This helps to explain why a fusion machine cannot explode like a hydrogen bomb, which also works by fusing deuterons and tritons. In a hydrogen bomb, the mixture is contained in a lithium-hydride solid and is heated in a few billionths of a second by the explosion of an atomic bomb. All the fusion energy is released in another few billionths of a second, and the mixture explodes. In a fusion machine, the energy release is, relatively speaking, very slow—so slow that no explosion can take place. The plasma is heated fairly slowly by electric power, and then it must be held together for at least a second by the magnetic fields so that the fusion energy will compensate for the energy that has gone into heating the plasma. In the sun, gravity holds the plasma together for billions of years, and therefore weak processes like the fusion of two protons to make a deuteron, a positron, and a neutrino produce energy, but these processes are too slow to be of any use in producing energy in an apparatus like a TOKAMAK.

The deuteron-triton plasma that future fusion power reactors will require as fuel poses a problem. The triton is unstable, having a half-life of twelve and a half years. Thus, it occurs as a natural isotope only in very minute quantities, and must be manufactured. The manufacturing will be done by bombarding lithium with neutrons, to produce a triton and a helium nucleus. If part of the blanket in a future TOKAMAK power reactor is made of lithium, tritons will be manufactured as the machine operates; like a breeder, it will produce fuel as it goes along. It would, however, be much better to use pure deuterium as the fuel, for deuterium can be extracted from seawater; it is not radioactive and so is simpler to handle; and there is enough in the sea to supply our needs for the next ten billion years. The trouble is that this pure deuteron plasma does not "ignite" until it reaches a temperature of about three hundred million degrees, compared to a hundred million for the deuteron-triton mixture, so it may be that it will come into use only after scientists have learned to make a fusion machine that produces power with the deuteron-triton mixture. While fusion does take place in the present generation of experimental machines, all of them consume much more power than they produce. It is hoped that the next generation of machines will begin to break even in power, and that fusion power will eventually become a practical possibility. With all the ancillary equipment, the new experimental machines now cost hundreds of millions of dollars, but that investment will pay off handsomely if we can learn to make electrical power from seawater. It may also be possible to use these machines to breed new fissionable material by surrounding them with blankets of thorium, which the escaping energetic neutrons can convert into U-233. Hopeful as some people may be about the prospects for fusion, however, it cannot be counted on to make a contribution to our energy problem within the next few decades.

A number of people who have pondered the energy question feel that solar energy may help solve our energy problem in the near future. In Bethe's view, solar energy may help to some extent by the year 2000, but even then its contribution will be relatively small. Wishful thinking about solar energy, he feels, should not be allowed to dominate our consideration of the energy problem to the extent that we fail to develop those sources of energy which *can* make a decisive contribution. "The best way to use sunlight is the way that mankind has used it for ten thousand years; namely, to grow grains and forests, and to use the grains to feed ourselves and our animals, and to use the forests for building, paper, and the rest," Bethe told me. "But that is not what people have in mind when they talk about solar energy. They have in mind two things. One is its use for heating houses and for heating water, and the other is its use in the production of electricity. I have looked into both of them quite closely, and I am sorry but I am quite negative about them. I like the sun—after all, I found out how the sun works. But after looking at the available evidence I do not believe that the sun will solve our problems—certainly not in the twentieth century. Maybe in the twenty-first. That I just don't know.

"The heating of water by solar radiation *is* a perfectly

feasible procedure. It would be economical in many parts of this country, and it is practiced in many places in Europe. The reason that heating water is more important than heating space is that one needs hot water all year; one can make use of solar heat in the summer, when there is lots of sunlight everywhere. Space heating by sunlight is economical today only under certain circumstances and in certain parts of the country. The first question is, how expensive are the solar panels? Currently, they cost something like fifteen dollars a square foot. It is possible that with mass production the cost could be brought down to something like seven dollars a square foot, but what really costs a lot of money is the rest of the system—the pipes going through the house, and the hot-water-storage facility one needs because the amount of sunlight is variable. Today may be a sunny day, but tomorrow may be terrible. In fact, the storage of heat is the main problem with the use of solar energy. If one wants to go completely solar, then the heat must be stored for a long time. Otherwise, the solar installation has to be supplemented by a conventional source, such as gas. Most solar-heating systems have a two-day or three-day storage capacity, and after that one has to fall back on the gas company. Generally, the solar people agree that a reasonable strategy would be to get half the heat from the sun and half from natural gas or some similar source. If one does this, and if one can get the panels and the ancillary equipment down to about seven dollars a square foot, then in some parts of this country solar heating will be dollar competitive with the *future* price of gas, natural or synthetic. Almost nowhere is it competitive with the present average price of natural gas, which costs the consumer three to four dollars per thousand cubic feet. This price probably won't last very long, and if we have to use synthetic gas—made from coal—rather than natural gas, it is likely to double, at least. If it does, there will be some parts of the country where solar heating will be economically advantageous. These are not the places one might expect. They are the Rocky Mountain area from New Mexico to Montana, and the coast of California. The reason is that these places get a lot of sunshine in the winter, when homes have to be heated. If one goes to Texas or Florida, one also has lots of sunshine in the winter, but one's home hardly ever needs heating. It should also be realized that the energy consumed in the manufacturing of solar installations is considerable, because all of them are rather bulky."

Bethe went on, "I have made a little calculation of what a private individual might do about solar heating. Others have made similar calculations, but mine may be somewhat simpler. A private individual has something else to worry about, and that is inflation. A private individual has no good way to protect himself against inflation, and in my calculation I take this fact into account. It turns out that if a person in one of the regions of the country that are favorable for solar heating buys one of the cheaper solar-heating units and it lasts for twenty years, he will be better off than if he puts the same amount of money in a savings account and then uses the interest to pay his heating-gas bill in the future. In making this calculation, I have assumed that the price of gas will increase at ten percent a year in real dollars until it reaches an average of seven dollars a thousand cubic feet. On this assumption, solar heating is a good investment. I do not think that the same thing applies to apartment houses or office buildings, because in these one does not have a large enough surface area to trap the required solar heat. But one must always keep in mind that at present only about ten percent of our energy consumption goes into the heating of private homes. Even if all the new houses that are going to be built between now and the year 2000 were equipped with solar heating, it would account for only about two percent of our energy consumption in that year. Still, a two percent saving of energy is worthwhile, because it is two percent of an enormous number. Though it will not solve our energy problem, it can contribute to a solution, and I am glad that so many people are working on it."

Bethe added, "By the way, Theodore Taylor, the Princeton physicist, has come up with a nice idea that might, in the future, help quite a lot in solar heating. This has to do with heating not individual houses but a complex of, say, a hundred houses. His notion is to take advantage of seasonal heat storage. He would construct enormous pools of water, about a hundred metres on a side and ten metres deep—pools that are exposed to the sun's heat during the summer. One would cover these pools with plastic, so that the stored heat would not be lost by either evaporation or radiation. In the winter, one could use this heat by piping the water into the complex of houses. The idea appeals to me, and I hope it works. But one must keep in mind that it is at present untested and that it would apply, in its present form, only to places where the population density is rather small. One must set aside an area about the size of a small park just for a pool. It would take some time to install these facilities, but if enough space is available one might be able to make communal solar-heating facilities at prices competitive with the present price of natural gas."
In the winter of 1980 Taylor got a small grant from the Prudential Insurance Company to finance a pilot project to make solar ponds in Princeton. The first pond, which is lo-

cated not far from the giant Princeton Plasma Physics Laboratory, is fifteen feet deep and sixty square feet across the top, and looks somewhat like a large square pail. This pond was built to demonstrate solar air conditioning. It held one thousand two hundred tons of ice during the winter months; the notion being that with the insulation this would produce a pond of water suitable for cooling even in summer. A second pond is to be built which, in principle, will store, for the winter months, warm water manufactured in the summer. If it works the Prudential Company will use the system to heat and cool its new building, and it is estimated that in two years the savings in fuel costs could pay off the entire investment. It still remains to be seen whether the scheme will really work.

"This is about the best idea I have heard of for using solar energy on a large scale," Bethe said. "When it comes to the prospects for making electricity from solar heat—either for a small community or for a large central power station— things look a great deal worse. The development that I have studied is the one that is now going on in Barstow, California. Four teams are participating. Each team consists of a big industrial firm, an architect-engineering firm, a research group, and a utility. They are constructing what is known as a power tower. This is the cheapest way that has so far been proposed to produce electricity from solar radiation. It consists of one tower—perhaps a hundred metres high—surrounded by a field of about eighteen hundred heliostats, or movable mirrors. Each mirror is a square six and a half metres on a side. The mirrors are individually directed by a computer during the day so that they continuously reflect the maximum solar radiation on the central tower. This heats water in the tower, and the boiling water is fed into a standard electricity generator. It is estimated that with the current technology the power tower can produce electricity at a price of two or three thousand dollars per peak installed kilowatt—"peak" meaning the sun at midday. In this price estimate, all the savings on mass production of the mirrors have been figured in. Moreover, the kilowatts are available only in the daytime and possibly a few hours afterward—with suitable heat storage —while nuclear power is available twenty-four hours a day. This means that one kilowatt of installed nuclear power is equivalent to about two kilowatts of installed solar power. The power tower might produce electricity at about four times the cost of nuclear power. A system like that is practical only in a desert, because the areas involved are very large—about eight square miles to produce as much power (one gigawatt) as the standard nuclear or coal-fired plant—and one would not want to divert such areas from agricultural production. If one wanted to supply all our electrical power this way, one would need about eighty million mirrors, covering an area of almost five thousand square miles. Such an array could be accommodated in our Western deserts and also in many tropical countries, but it would be difficult to find similar areas in Europe or Japan, even if reliable sunshine were available there. The environmental effects have not yet been assessed. At the estimated mass-production prices, five thousand square miles of mirror and their generating stations would represent an investment of nine hundred billion dollars. Our present rate of investment in power stations is about twenty billion dollars a year, and at that rate it would take forty years to install enough solar power stations to supply even our present needs—and, of course, the first station would have broken down before the last one was built."

Much of the interest in the use of solar energy is centered

on what are known as photovoltaic devices, or solar cells. These have been used to provide electric power for spacecraft. In the space program, economics was not a consideration, whereas economics is the primary consideration in large-scale terrestrial applications. First, how do these devices work? When light of sufficient energy illuminates a material like silicon or germanium, the electrons that are always present in the material can be promoted, energetically, into what is known as the conduction band. These electrons can then flow, and the resulting current is available for useful work. It turns out that only a relatively narrow part of the solar spectrum is useful for exciting the electrons. When the sunlight is below a minimum energy, the electrons cannot be induced to flow, and above a certain energy a significant portion of the light energy is dissipated in useless heat. This limits the theoretical efficiency of the cells. A silicon cell has a maximum theoretical efficiency of about twenty-nine percent, while a gallium arsenide cell has about a thirty-six percent efficiency. A recent study on solar-photovoltaic energy by the American Physical Society notes that ingenious combinations of materials might produce a maximal efficiency greater than fifty percent; but the more complex the arrangement, the more it will cost to make. In practice, the limitations on the working efficiency of the cells are considerably below the theoretical maximum, because of imperfections in the cells. Present-day cells convert sunlight into electricity with an overall efficiency of about ten percent. Because of this the present collectors are very large. It requires about sixteen square feet of solar panel to generate 170 watts—enough to light a large lightbulb under peak conditions.

What, then, would the cost of photovoltaic electricity have to be in order to be competitive with, say, coal-generated electricity in the year 2000? The American Physical Society study concluded that, so far as cost was concerned, it did not matter significantly whether the cells were used in a central power station or whether they were deployed residentially. In either case, to be competitive their price would have to be between ten and forty cents (in 1975 dollars) per generated watt. (The analysis is done for peak wattage—when the sun is shining at its brightest. Evidently, the cells will generate no electricity when the sun is not shining. This means that the photocells will have to be implemented with an electrical storage system such as a battery. There is nothing now in view that would lower the price of storage to where it is comparable to the target price of the cells.) In other words, the price would have to come down by a factor of about twenty. In a discussion of the study, published in *Physics Today*, Henry Ehrenreich, the study group's chairman, and his colleague John Martin note, "This requirement is sufficiently stringent as to require major technical advances, if not breakthroughs, before extensive deployment can become a reasonable course of action." They worry that "a premature entry into large-scale U.S. deployment before the technology has reached fruition might lock us into an overly costly technology. Indeed, the national interest may well be served optimally by an emphasis on research and development accompanied by measured and technologically appropriate progress in government-assisted commercialization." They conclude that it will be "some thirty years or more" before photovoltaics can make a real dent in our energy problems.

When I discussed this report with Bethe, he commented, "Photovoltaic devices, which convert solar radiation directly into electric current, have become much cheaper in the last few years, and a lot of research is going on in this field, but they are still at least three times the price of the power tower. Perhaps their price will come down in the future, but we cannot count on that. The use of satellites for collecting solar energy and beaming it down by microwaves to earth is, as far as I can see, far more expensive still, because of the cost of transporting all the materials up into space. Windmills have been proposed as an indirect way of harnessing the sun's energy; they may have their uses in certain regions, where winds are strong and steady, especially if the regions are also very remote—such as the Aleutian Islands, where it is costly to bring in conventional energy sources. But on the whole wind-generated power is high-cost power compared to conventional sources, and, in any case, it is not very reliable." *

Bethe went on, "As you can see, I have been rather negative about solar energy in this discussion. That does not mean that I am against using solar energy—on the contrary. Wherever it is economically reasonable, it is a very good thing to use. The trouble that I have with proposals to use solar energy is that so many people promise that it will by itself solve our energy problem. It won't—or, at least, there is nothing now in sight to indicate that it will. It will contribute here and there to the heating of water, to the heating of houses, and possibly to some industrial heating. For instance, solar heat could be used for the drying

---

* To get a sense of scale, a highly efficient windmill driven by a wind of twenty miles per hour can generate about one hundred and eighty watts per square metre of wind-gathering surface. This means that if the wind surface of each mill were, say, a hundred square metres it would take about fifty thousand of such windmills to produce the billion watts equivalent to a large nuclear power plant. The wattage increases with the cube of the wind velocity, but there are not many places with average winds as high or higher than twenty miles per hour.

of vegetables or the generating of "process heat"—that is, utilizing hot water for industrial purposes. But our need for energy is much too great to be satisfied this way, and the production of solar electricity on a large scale is as yet nowhere in sight. Therefore, what I am troubled about with solar energy is that people use it as an excuse, a reason for not developing other sources of energy—primarily nuclear and coal—which we know how to use, and which, in combination, could satisfy our energy needs. To postpone and slow down the use of these important sources of energy because of some distant future in which solar energy may become very important seems to me a dangerous thing for our country and for the world. I am not against solar energy. Let us do all the research we can on it. Let us use it in every way that is economically feasible. But let us not use it as an argument against taking energy measures that are more immediate and necessary."

Epilogue: Policy Options

IN the light of Bethe's over-all analysis, I asked him what he felt the country should be doing to deal with the energy problem. What specific steps should we be taking now?

"First of all, the country has to realize that the energy problem is terribly serious and is likely to be permanent," he answered. "Next, it must recognize that there are really two problems: one is to provide enough *total* energy, and the other is to provide fluid fuels of all types—mainly oil and gas. But for the next twenty years, at least, I believe that the mainstays will have to be coal and nuclear power —that we will need more of both of them. Much more. We should make every effort to get more coal, not only from our Eastern mines but also from our Western mines. I do not think that this is a time when we should favor one kind of mine over the other. We will need them all, and we will need to open Western mines, in particular, rather quickly. We will have to rebuild our railroads so that in the future we can transport coal from our Western mines. We should replace oil with coal in the production of electric power as soon as possible. The use of so much coal will require us to adopt a more flexible attitude toward the pollution problems that coal produces. For example, Western coal is largely free of sulfur, so power plants that use it should not need the elaborate scrubbers required for plants that use Eastern coal. These scrubbers, which remove the sulfur from the smoke, add about a hundred million dollars to the cost of a coal-burning power plant. There will have to be some give and take between the obvious need to prevent air pollution and the equally obvious need to conserve oil. Coal should be substituted for oil wherever possible in electric power plants and in industrial heating. Coal can also serve as a raw material for solving the second problem, that of providing fluid fuels—synthetic gas and oil. It is believed that synthetic gas can be made for about five dollars per thousand cubic feet—a price that is equivalent in heating value to about a thirty dollar barrel of oil, which is not very far from the present world-market oil price. Synthetic oil from coal would be more expensive. Luckily, for this purpose we have an alternative—shale oil, which can be distilled from certain rocks. We have a great deal of oil shale, especially in Colorado and Utah, and we should begin to exploit these deposits.

"The prospects for synthetic gas and oil look rather hopeful. Both the President and Congress want to sponsor an effort to develop synthetic-fuel plants, both from coal and from oil shale. The plan is similar to one that was proposed in 1975 by Vice-President Nelson Rockefeller; namely, to set up a special energy fund for lending money for such investments. We have lost four precious years, but now that the urgency is more obvious I hope this plan will materialize quickly. The oil will be needed to replace natural petroleum for running cars, trucks, diesel locomotives, and airplanes, and both oil and gas are essential for making the petrochemicals that are basic for so many of our industrial products.

"We clearly need to improve the safety of our nuclear reactors. One of the lessons that Three Mile Island taught us was that the signals on the control panel of a reactor must be improved so as to give the operators a clear picture of the state of the reactor at all times. Reactor operators must be better trained and better paid, and the weaknesses in some of the specific reactor designs must be corrected. The accident also appears to have convinced the nuclear industry to take some strong new steps to improve reactor safety. It is not just a matter of improving the industry's public image. The financial losses in an accident like that at Three Mile Island, even when there is no substantial effect on the health of individuals, are enormous. In every way, the industry simply cannot afford to have accidents like that. There are three major new programs—the Nuclear Safety Analysis Center, the Institute for Nuclear Power Operations, and a mutual-insurance program to help individual electric utilities in case there is an accident. In my view, the most important of the new entities is the Institute for Nuclear Power Operations. In addition to setting educational and training requirements for nuclear-power-plant operators, it will also conduct independent evaluations to assist utilities in meeting the standards it sets.

III / Prophet of Energy

Very likely, participation in this program will be a condition for inclusion in the mutual-insurance program. So there will be strong incentives for individual utilities to meet high standards of safety and excellence in reactor operation. I feel sure that through the joint efforts of industry and government nuclear safety in the future will be much greater than it has been and that the probability of a major accident can be reduced to a very low level indeed—much lower still than the estimates in the Rasmussen report."

Summing up, Bethe said, "Aside from improving nuclear safety, we must also start serious efforts toward the disposal of nuclear wastes. In particular, we must make a systematic geological study of places that might be suitable for waste disposal. Large amounts of nuclear waste exist now—some four thousand tons of it from civilian reactors and an even greater amount from the military program—and it will not go away by wishful thinking. We must also understand that uranium, like oil, is a vanishing resource. Hence, we should develop reactors like the CANDU, which use less uranium for the generation of a given amount of power than our present power plants do. I think that—for the next few decades, at least—nuclear power is essential for our energy needs. But it is not enough to solve our energy problems. We need a determined conservation effort, especially in transportation and in the insulation of houses. We must start to conserve now. We need a vigorous program to make synthetic fuels, and it now seems that the government will inaugurate such a program. Research and development of solar energy should be encouraged, although I do not believe it will make a substantial impact in the next twenty years or so. No one of these programs by itself will solve our energy problems, but all of them together have a good chance of succeeding."

Glossary

THIS GLOSSARY is not meant to be a complete compendium of the technical terms used in this book. It is, rather, an amplification of those terms and concepts that seem to cause trouble for the interested layman.

Chain reaction—When a heavy nucleus, like uranium, splits, or fissions, among the final products are one or more neutrons. (See "neutron".) These neutrons are then available for further uranium fissions. These sequential processes are known as a chain reaction. At a certain mass, known as the critical mass of the material, this process becomes self-sustaining. For U-235 the critical mass is about twenty kilograms and for plutonium it is about six kilograms.

Glossary

Electron—This is the particle with the least mass known to carry an electric charge. A neutral atom has a central massive nucleus made up of neutrons and protons. At a very great distance, considering the size of this nucleus, there is a "cloud" of electrons sufficient in number to render the atom, as a whole, electrically neutral.

Energy—In the body of the text I have attempted to explain how the term energy is used in physics. I now wish to describe the different, and often very confusing, units in which energy is measured. In this book I have decided, after much soul searching, to present energies as we often use them in household practice in the unit *kilowatthours*. The reason for this is that we all have some experience in paying energy bills in terms of this unit. Most of us never deal, in practice, with units such as *electron volts* or *quads*. However, both of these units, and others, do appear in the literature on this subject. Hence I offer a translation table of these units with a few additional comments. The table is read from left to right: *1 kilowatt-hour* equals *x calories*, and so on. To go backwards one divides. I belabor these, perhaps elementary, matters because a good deal of the rather loose talk about energy has its origin—or so it seems to me—in the unfamiliar and intimidating numbers and units by which energy is measured, which make it difficult for many people to think quantitatively about the subject. To put things into perspective one might keep in mind that the human body dissipates about 100 watt hours of energy per hour. There is an additional complication which has been alluded to in the text. Electric bills are given in terms of kilowatt hours electric. The kilowatt hours below are so-called thermal kilowatt hours. These are three times as large and do not take into account the loss

Glossary

due to efficiency when one burns oil or coal to make electricity. Thus:

1 kilowatt-hour = 3413 British Thermal Units (BTU) = 1.34 horse power—hours = 8.6×10^5 calories = 2.25×10^{25} electron volts

A very common unit that is used in discussions of the energy question is the so-called *quad*. A quad is a quadrillion, or 10^{15} BTUs. This somewhat bizarre unit plays the same role in a discussion of energy as the *light year* does in astronomy. It enables one to replace very large numbers by smaller ones defined in terms of units that are themselves very large. To see how this works, let us translate our total energy consumption per year, which is about 22.5×10^{12} kilowatt hours, into quads. Thus:

22.5×10^{12} kilowatt hours = $3413 \times 22.5 \times 10^{12}$ BTU = 76.8 quads.

The rest of the world uses about 225 quads. As I have mentioned in the text, the energy content of one barrel of oil, or 42 gallons, is equivalent to about 1700 kilowatt hours. It should also be apparent from the discussion that a kilowatt by itself is *not* a unit of energy. It is, rather, a unit in which the rate of energy flow is measured. These energy rates are what is meant by *power*. A kilowatt is, therefore, a unit of power.

Fission—This refers to the process of "splitting" a heavy nucleus, like that of the uranium atom, into less massive fragments. A typical fission reaction is one in which, say, a slow neutron splits a nucleus of U-235 into a cesium and a rubidium nucleus, with the emission of three neutrons. This can be described by the equation:

$$N + U\text{-}235 \rightarrow Cs\text{-}140 + Rb\text{-}93 + 3\,N$$

The reader will notice that the number of nuclear particles, protons and neutrons, is the same on both sides of the equation: 236. The electric charge is also conserved. U-235 has 92 protons and hence a positive charge of 92 units. The neutron has no charge. Cesium has a charge of 55 units while rubidium has a charge of 37 units, and $55 + 37 = 92$.

Fusion—This is a nuclear reaction in which two light nuclei combine to produce one, or more, different light particles and the release of energy. A typical fusion reaction which may someday be useful for Power Production is:

$$D + D \rightarrow He^3 + N$$

Here D stands for "deuteron" (see also "isotope"), P for proton, He^3 for a light isotope of helium, and N for a neutron.

Isotope—The atomic nucleus consists of neutrons and protons. The number of protons indirectly determines the chemical properties of the atom, since this number is balanced by an equal number of electrons that do determine the chemistry. If one adds or subtracts neutrons from the nucleus the atomic chemistry will remain similar since the number of protons remains the same. These related nuclei are known as isotopes. In this book the isotopes listed below play an especially important role. To denote a given isotope, I have employed, according to convenience, two notations. Thus, U^{235} and U-235 stand for the same isotope of uranium. The more important isotopes of hydrogen are:

P (proton)—the nucleus of ordinary hydrogen
D (deuteron)—a proton and a neutron
T (triton)—a proton with two neutrons

These can also be symbolized by H, H^2, and H^3. In the discussion of solar physics two isotopes of helium play a role: He^3 and He^4. He^4 is the common isotope with two neutrons and two protons, while He^3 has one neutron. In discussing fission, various isotopes of uranium and plutonium must be considered. As has been mentioned, U-235 has 92 protons and 143 neutrons. The reader will have no trouble in listing the constituents of, say, U-238. The plutonium nucleus Pu-239 has 94 protons and 145 neutrons; knowing this it is a straightforward proposition to adduce the constitution of the other plutonium isotopes.

Moderator—It is a basic fact of nuclear physics that the rate for fission of U-235 greatly increases when neutrons are slowed down. U-238, however, will only fission when it is bombarded by fast neutrons. Conventional power reactors produce energy when slow neutrons cause U-235 or plutonium to fission. But since these fissions produce fast neutrons they must be slowed down in order to make the reactor work. This is the role of the moderator—a substance with which neutrons can collide and lose energy. Among the substances that have been used as moderators are sodium, graphite, ordinary water, and heavy water, which is made of deuterium and oxygen. Heavy water is such an effective moderator that natural uranium can be used in reactors that employ it.

Neutrino—This is a remarkable particle that is emitted

when many unstable nuclei spontaneously disintegrate. The neutrino—or really neutrinos, since there is more than one type—has no charge and as far as is known no mass, although the most recent experiments suggest it might have a tiny mass. For each neutrino there is an associated *anti-neutrino*; this is also a chargeless, and perhaps massless particle which, nonetheless, can be distinguished from its partner. At the present time it is believed that there are three distinct types of neutrino, each with an anti-neutrino partner. In this book I have been concerned with the so-called *electron-neutrino*, and its anti-particle—the type that is emitted in common radioactive decays. The prototype of such a decay is that of the neutron which decays into: a proton, an electron e^-, and an anti-electron neutrino $\bar{\nu}_e$. Symbolically:

$$N \rightarrow P + e^- + \bar{\nu}_e$$

On the average a neutron decays in fifteen minutes. This time is known as its *mean* life.

Neutron—The neutron is the massive electrically neutral particle which, with the proton, composes the atomic nucleus. Its mass is about two thousand times that of the electron. It was discovered in 1932 by the British physicist James Chadwick.

Plasma—Plasmas are sometimes referred to as the fourth state of matter; the other three being solid, liquid, and gas. As has been mentioned, a neutral atom consists of a cloud of electrons that surround the positively charged atomic nucleus. If the atoms are subject to high temperatures, for example, in the interior of a star, the electrons get knocked off in the frequent collisions between the atoms. This pro-

Glossary

duces a substance—a plasma—which consists of free electrons and *ions*. (Ions are charged atoms with too few electrons to maintain electrical neutrality.) On earth the plasma state is produced under experimental conditions in the laboratory; hence it is easy to overlook the fact that in nature plasmas are quite common; in fact, the interiors of stars are plasmas.

Positron—The positron is the anti-particle of the electron. It has the same mass as the electron and an equal charge of opposite sign. When electrons and positrons encounter one another they may mutually annihilate into gamma rays—very energetic quanta of electromagnetic radiation. Positrons were anticipated on theoretical grounds by P.A.M. Dirac a few years before their discovery in 1932. The *anti-proton* bears the same relation to the proton that the positron bears to the electron. It is the negatively charged counterpart of the proton and it was observed experimentally in 1955.

Proton—This is the charged component of the atomic nucleus. It carries the same charge as the electron in magnitude but of the opposite sign. It is slightly less massive than the neutron. Until recently, it was universally believed that the proton was absolutely stable. It is now conjectured that while the proton is extremely long-lived it may also spontaneously decay. Lest one worry about the stability of ordinary matter new theories predict a proton lifetime of about 10^{31} years. The age of the universe meanwhile is theorized to be only about 10^{10} years.

Quantum Theory—There is mention in the book of both the "old" quantum theory and the modern version. The old quantum theory was largely the work of Niels Bohr. According to Bohr, when atoms are energetically excited they give off light in the form of well-defined spectral lines, or definite colors. He attributed this to the fact that electrons can jump from one orbit to another. Thus, when an electron jumps from a high orbit to a lower one it looses energy, and this energy appears as quanta of electromagnetic radiation. Bohr's idea was that the electron orbits are restricted, or quantised, and he correlated these "allowed" orbits with the observed atomic spectra. Bohr's theory was "classical" in the sense that the electrons are visualized as following classical orbits, in the manner of planets orbiting the sun. The modern quantum theory, which evolved out of the work of Heisenberg, Schrödinger, and Dirac, abandons the idea of classical orbits. In this theory, which was developed in the nineteen-twenties, one computes, for example, the probability of finding an electron at some location in an atom. This probability is given in terms of a so-called "wave function". In this sense, particles also have a wave nature—something that was first suggested by de Broglie. The abandoning of the classical orbits was not done out of a whim, but was a consequence of a far-reaching analysis of what measurement means when carried out on the atomic scale. The limitations of such measurement are what has been formalized in the so-called Heisenberg uncertainty relations.

Temperature—The most commonly employed temperature scales are Fahrenheit, centigrade or Celsius, and absolute or Kelvin. The Fahrenheit scale, which is almost never used in scientific work, is based on taking, arbitrarily, the freezing point of water at $32°F$ and the boiling point at $212°F$. In the centrigrate scale these points are $0°C$ and $100°C$ respectively. The connection between these two scales is given by the equation:

$$t_c = 5/9(t_f - 32).$$

The so-called *absolute zero* of temperature is the lowest possible temperature. This is $-459.69°F$ or $-273.15°C$. The Kelvin scale fixes this point at $0°K$. To go from Kelvin to centigrade 273.15 is subtracted from the Kelvin temperature.

Bibliography

Bernstein, Jeremy. *Experiencing Science*. New York: Basic Books, 1978. This book contains a profile of I. I. Rabi which complements that of Bethe.

Beyerchen, Alan D. *Scientists Under Hitler*. New Haven: Yale, 1977. Professor Beyerchen has made a definitive study of the relationship between German science and the Third Reich.

Blumberg, Stanley, A., and Gwinn Owens. *Energy and Conflict, The Life and Times of Edward Teller*. New York: Putnam, 1976. This is said to be Teller's preferred biography.

Boorse, Henry A., and Lloyd Motz. *The World of the Atom*. New York: Basic Books, 1966. This fine annotated collection of articles about atomic physics contains two of Bethe's most important papers.

Butti, Ken, and Perlin John. *A Golden Thread*. Palo Alto: Cheshire Books, 1980. A delightful history of the use of solar energy from the Greeks to the present.

Bibliography

Dyson, Freeman. *Disturbing The Universe*. New York: Harper & Row, 1979. The author gives us a picture of Bethe, the teacher of physics.

Foster, Arthur R., and Robert L. Wright Jr. *Basic Nuclear Engineering*. Boston: Allyn and Bacon, 1977. This is a solid textbook in nuclear engineering for people who want to learn more about how reactors work.

Groueff, Stephane. *Manhattan Project*. Boston: Little Brown, 1967. A colorful account about the making of the atomic bomb.

Irving, David. *The German Atomic Bomb*. New York: Simon & Schuster, 1967. An excellent account of the attempt by the Germans to make an atomic bomb and why it failed.

Marshak, Robert E. *Perspectives in Modern Physics*. New York: John Wiley, 1966. This is Bethe's "birthday book"; essays collected in honor of Bethe's sixtieth birthday. In addition there is a bibliography of Bethe's papers.

Oppenheimer, J. Robert. *In the Matter of J. Robert Oppenheimer*. Cambridge: M.I.T., 1971. This is a complete transcript of Oppenheimer's hearing. Much of it reads like a great drama.

Robert Oppenheimer: Letters and Recollections, edited by Alice Kimball Smith and Charles Weiner. Cambridge: Harvard University Press, 1980. This annotated collection is the nearest thing to a biography of Oppenheimer that is available.

Schmidt, Fred H., and Bodansky, David. *The Fight Over Nuclear Power*. San Francisco: Albion, 1976. A very informative short book on all aspects of nuclear power. Bethe wrote the foreword.

Thirring, Hans. *Energy for Man*. New York: Harper & Row, 1962. A clear general presentation of the phenomenon of energy.

Index

Index

Index

Index

Index

as a Jew, 8, 34; and Dachau, 37; and emigration of Jews, 38, 40, 51; and Heisenberg, 74–77 passim; Hitler as chancellor, 34; Hitler-Stalin Pact, 65–66; and invasion of Russia, 66; Jews in, 34, 39; Meitner's escape from, 68; and the Ministry of Cultural Affairs, 35; and science, 36–38, 75; *Scientists Under Hitler*, 36; and Sommerfeld, 35, 36; and the Swastika, 33; Vemork hydroelectric plant, 76

Nazi socialist Organization, 33

Negative hydrogen ion (H-minus), 24

Neutrino, 47, 53, 120, 197–98

Neutron, 42, 198; absorbtion in light- and heavy-water reactors, 165; bombardment of nucleus by, 67; and electron volts, 130; in breeder reactor, 166; and Fermi's experiments, 67; and fission, 130, 132, 163; and the sun, 120

New York Academy of Sciences, 51

Nixon, Richard M., 105, 106

Nobel Prize, 19, 42–43, 61, 66, 90; and Bethe on stellar energy, 4; and expatriated German scientists, 36; and students of Sommerfeld, 13; winners invited to the White House, 101

Nuclear energy: attitudes toward, 161; Bethe on, 88, 102; and concern about safety, 135–36, 137, 155; control of, 88; and controversy about technology, 127; European commitment to, 169; international standards for, 155; peaceful use of, 102; safety program, 191; society's need for, 136; use of, 159

Nuclear fission, 195; attitudes toward, 69, 70; and binding energy, 130; bombardment by neutrons, 67; in a breeder reactor, 166; chain reaction, 69, 83–84, 71; discovery of, 66, 68; and electron volts, 130; in heavy-water reactor, 163–65; and irradiation, 67; and isotope separation in, 70; in light-water reactor, 163; and liquid-drop model, 67–69; in nuclear reactors, 124; neutrons in, 130, 132, 163; and plutonium, 72–73; protons in, 132; and Nazi Germany, 73, 76; in stars, 48; and uranium, 69, 130, 132

Nuclear fusion, 52, 196–97; compared to carbon cycle, 50; and energy crisis, 179; as an energy source, 126; rate of, in hydrogen, 48; and stars, 49;

and the sun, 47, 119–20; and temperature, 48, 49; water in, 132

Nuclear fusion reactor, 174–78; *see also* TOKAMAK

Nuclear power plant, 128, 155, 159, 161

Nuclear reactors, 127, 191; accident potential in, 128, 140–42; Bethe on safety in, 138; Bethe as consultant to A. E. C. on, 102; containment building for, 128; controversy over, 127; cooling system in, 139; cost of, 123, 126; fission process in; *see* Nuclear fission; fissionable waste from, 124; fuel rods in, 129, 130, 132; and graphite, 132; heat from fission products in, 145; as a heat source, 127; heavy water in, 132, 164; and kinetic energy, 120, licensing of, 151; light water in, 163; loss of energy in, 159; moderators in, 164, 197; potential dangers, 138; refueling of, 164; reprocessing waste from, 162; and safeguards; *see* Safeguards in nuclear reactors; solar electric plant or, 184; and uranium in, 123–24, 129, 164; water in, 130, 131–32, 139; *see also* Boiling-water reactor; Breeder-reactor; Heavy-water reactor; Light-water reactor; Meltdown; Nuclear fusion reactor; Pressurized-water reactor

Nuclear Regulatory Commission (formerly Atomic Energy Commission), 146; Hendrie as chairman of, 146; Office of Reactor Regulation of, 145; and President's Commission, 151; power plant accidents, 138; and safety of nuclear plants, 155; technical help available to, 151; and Three Mile Island accident, 145–46

Nuclear strength, 87–89, 153–54, 161, 162

Nuclear technology, 127, 161, 162

Nuclear tests; *see* Atomic weapons testing

Nuclear test ban, 107–112

Nuclear theory and Bethe, 6

Office of Scientific Research and Development, 72, 88

Oil: Bethe on the Arab embargo, 116; cost of, 116, 117; for electricity, 170; for heating, 171; and pollution, 173; from shale, 190; and U.S. production of, 122; viscosity of, 123; world use and production of, 122–23

Index

Old quantum theory, 12, 13, 16, 17, 199–200; de Broglie's adaptation of, 17; faults in, 13
One World or None, 88
Oppenheimer, J. Robert: Acheson-Lilienthal Report and, 88; and the American Physical Society, 65; Bethe's relationship with, 65, 78, 101; as chairman of the General Advisory Committee, 94; and Chevalier incident, 98; as director of the Manhattan Project at Los Alamos, 60, 72, 78, 88; Enrico Fermi Award to, 101; and the H-bomb, 98; at the Institute for Advanced Study, 93; and Office of Scientific Research and Development, 72; on post-war use of nuclear strength, 87; *Robert Oppenheimer: Letters on Recollections*, 88n; and security clearance hearings, 97–101; Teller's relationship with, at Los Alamos, 81; and the White House, 101

Parsons, William (Captain), 81
Particle theory, (charged), 26, 27
Patterson, A. L., 20
Papen, Franz von, 34
Pauli exclusion principle, 36–37
Pauli, Wolfgang, 13, 21, 36–37
Pauling, Linus, 14
Peierls, Genia (nee Kannegiesser), 41–42
Photosphere and the sun, 24
Photovoltaics, 185–86
Physical Review, 46, 52
Physical Society, 12
Physics; *see* Experimental physics; Theoretical physics
Physics Today, 186
Plasma, 198–99
Planck's constant, 17
Plutonium: availability of, 70, 156–57; and bomb, 156; in a breeder reactor, 166; critical mass of, 83; discovery of, 81; and fission, 72–73; in fuel rods, 133; and Hanford Reactor, 87; and health, 133–34; and isolation from fuel rods, 156, 157; isotopes of, 156; manufacture of, 70; reactor production of, 124, 156; storage of, 134; use of, in nuclear weapons, 72–73
Plutonium bomb, 34, 87
Positron, 47, 120, 199
Power, 195

President's Medal of Merit, 6
President's Science Advisory Committee, and the study of ABMs, 105
Press, Frank, 105
Pressurized-water reactor, 127–30; cooling system in a, 142; cost of, 128; fission in a, 132; and fuel rods, 129; and problems with, 128; safeguards in a, 138, 139; and steam, 127, 142; and use of uranium-oxide, 129; and water as a moderator, 131–32
Princeton, 43, 60, 69, 82–83, 91, 93, 182
Princeton Plasma Physics Laboratory, 176
Proton, 47, 199; and chemistry of the atom, 70; and electron volts, 130; in fission, 132; in the sun, 120

Quads, 194, 195
Quantum-mechanics: Bethe on, 25, 33, 39; Bethe/Salpeter article on, 39–40; and exclusion principle, 37; and Feynman on electrons and protons using, 61; as invented by Heisenberg, 16; and hydrogen fusion, 48; and Hyllera's variational principle, 24; as a "Jewish invention," 37; and nuclei, 42; and wave mechanics, 15
Quantum theory, 13, 29, 49, 20; *see also* Old quantum theory

Rabi, I. I., 14, 62, 78, 80
Radar, 71, 72, 90, 105
Radiant energy in the sun, 119
Radiation Laboratory of M.I.T., 71
Radioactive decay, 119
Radioactive fallout, 149
Radioactive waste: Bethe on disposal of, 192; and Gabon study, 137; produced in a reactor, 124; reprocessing of, 156–57; storage of, 124; 132–35, 137, 157; and U.S. government on disposal sites, 135, 137, 161
Radioactivity: effect of, on the human body, 133–34, 149; measuring of, 33; release of, at power plants, 138, 154; in stored fuel rods, 133
Rasmussen report on reactor safety, 150
Reactor Division of the Department of Energy (Naval Branch), 165
Reprocessing plants: Bethe on Carter's program, 157; cost of heavy-water re-

2 1 0

Index

Index

Testing facilities, 139, 140, 87
Theoretical physics, 12, 13, 45; and Bethe, 5, 6
Thermal Kilowatts, 158
Thermonuclear weapons, 108
Third world nations, 153, 154
Thomson, G. P., 19
Thorium reactor, 165
Three Mile Island: accident at, 137, 143–46; aftermath at, 150–52; Bethe on, 147–51; and future reactor safety, 150; Governor Thornburgh and, 145, 146; human error at, 140, 142, 143, 144; and media response, 147; and Metropolitan Edison, 153; and report of the President's Commission on the accident at Three Mile Island, 151–52; safety system at, 142
TOKAMAK (toroidal magnetic chamber) for a fusion reactor, 176–78
Tomonaga, Sinitro, 61, 90–91
Trasnsuranic elements, 133
Tritium, 176
Triton, 177, 178
Truman, Harry S. (President), 94

Ulam, Stanislaw, 95
United Nations: International Conference on the Peaceful Uses of Atomic Energy, 126; Russian veto of international control of atomic energy, 88
United States: and research of the A-bomb, 66, 69; and Bethe on energy options, 189–92; and decline of nuclear technology, 161; and Dresden nuclear power plant, 126; and energy crisis, 117; and thermonuclear weapons, 108; the United States Geological Survey's estimate of undiscovered oil, 123; and uses of energy, 130–59; and waste of nuclear fuel, 161
University of California at Berkeley, 65, 66, 72, 77, 79
University of Frankfurt, 9, 11, 12, 116
University of Manchester, 38, 40, 42
University of Munich, 13, 14, 25, 31–32
Uranium, 69, 79; and actinides in stored fuel rods, 133; Bethe's attitude toward, 131; in boiling water reactor, 129; and decline in nuclear power stations, 155; enrichment of, 129, 164; and

fission, 69, 130, 132; as fuel for reactors, 721; in heavy-water reactor, 164; supply of, 124, 128–29, 161; in nuclear reactors, 123–24, 129, 164; at Oak Ridge, 87; and ordinary power reactor, 84; in plutonium manufacture, 70; and seawater, 129

Variational principle and the atom, 24
Vitreous State Laboratory at Catholic University and research on containers for radioactive material, 134
Von Braun, Werner, 104
Von Kármán, Theodore, 64
Von Laue, Max, 13, 18–19
Van Vleck, John H., 42–43

Water injection system, 139
Water in a nuclear reactor, 130, 131–32, 139
Wave mechanics, 15, 16, 17, 19
Weisskopf, V. F., 5, 93
Weizäcker, C. F. von, 47, 50
Weizäcker-Bethe-Critchfield process, 50
Western Electric Company, 18
Wheeler, J. A., 69
Windscale reprocessing plant, 162
Wildt, R., 24
Windmills, 187, 187n
Winter, George, 61
Works by Bethe, 67; "Electronen-theorie de Metalle," 32; "Quantum Mechanics of One- and Two-Electron Atoms," 40; *Review of Modern Physics*, 44; "The Theory of the Passage of Swift Corpuscular Rays Through Matter," 25
World use of breeder reactor, 124, 167
X-ray diffraction theory of crystals, 18–20, 23

York, Herbert, 96

Zeitschrift für Physik, 31
Zinn, Walter, 69, 166
Zwicky, Fritz, 20